Advanced Gatsby Projects

Create Two Advanced Sites Using Technologies that Compliment Gatsby

Nabendu Biswas

Apress®

Advanced Gatsby Projects: Create Two Advanced Sites Using Technologies that Compliment Gatsby

Nabendu Biswas
Bangalore, India

ISBN-13 (pbk): 978-1-4842-6639-7   ISBN-13 (electronic): 978-1-4842-6640-3
https://doi.org/10.1007/978-1-4842-6640-3

Managing Director, Apress Media LLC: Welmoed Spahr
Acquisitions Editor: Louise Corrigan
Development Editor: James Markham
Coordinating Editor: Nancy Chen

Cover designed by eStudioCalamar

Cover image designed by Freepik (www.freepik.com)

Distributed to the book trade worldwide by Springer Science + Business Media New York, 1 New York Plaza, New York, NY 10004. Phone 1-800-SPRINGER, fax (201) 348-4505, e-mail orders-ny@springer-sbm.com, or visit www.springeronline.com. Apress Media, LLC is a California LLC and the sole member (owner) is Springer Science + Business Media Finance Inc (SSBM Finance Inc). SSBM Finance Inc is a **Delaware** corporation.

For information on translations, please e-mail booktranslations@springernature.com; for reprint, paperback, or audio rights, please e-mail bookpermissions@springernature.com.

Apress titles may be purchased in bulk for academic, corporate, or promotional use. eBook versions and licenses are also available for most titles. For more information, reference our Print and eBook Bulk Sales web page at http://www.apress.com/bulk-sales.

Any source code or other supplementary material referenced by the author in this book is available to readers on GitHub via the book's product page, located at www.apress.com/9781484266397. For more detailed information, please visit http://www.apress.com/source-code.

Printed on acid-free paper

To my Dad. I miss him every day! He left for heaven in November 2020 due to a stroke. He had retired 10 years back from a top government organization, BHEL, as a senior engineer. He always was the pillar in my life. I hoped to spend more time with him, but life had some other plans.

Table of Contents

About the Author

Nabendu Biswas is a full-stack JavaScript developer who has been working in the information technology industry for the past 15 years. He has worked for some of the world's top development firms and investment banks. He is currently working as an Associate Architect at Innominds. He is a passionate tech blogger who publishes on thewebdev.tech. He is a tech YouTuber with a channel named The Web Dev, and also loves to teach people web development. He is an all-around nerd, passionate about everything JavaScript, React, and Gatsby. You can find him on Twitter: @nabendu82.

About the Technical Reviewer

Alexander Chinedu Nnakwue has a background in mechanical engineering from the University of Ibadan, Nigeria, and has been a front-end developer for more than three years, working on both web and mobile technologies. He also has experience as a technical author, writer, and reviewer. He enjoys programming for the Web, and occasionally, you can also find him playing soccer. He was born in Benin City and is currently based in Lagos, Nigeria.

Introduction

This book contains two advanced Gatsby projects and it is advisable for beginners to Gatsby to start with my book *Foundation Gatsby Projects*. In the first project, we will create a fully functional e-commerce site for a restaurant using Snipcart. Through this, site a user can place an order and also pay via credit card. It also has a nice dashboard and email notification for the owner of the restaurant.

In the second project, you will learn to build a recipe site using the awesome and free-to-use Firebase real-time database. With Firebase we can use a back end without complicated back ends like Java or NodeJS. We are also going to add a commenting system in this project with Disqus.

PART I

Creating an Ecommerce Feature Site with Snipcart

In Part I, we will build a restaurant site with GatsbyJS. This site will also have an ecommerce feature that allows users to order online. We will be using Snipcart for this feature. We are also going to deploy the project in Netlify and store the data in the Contentful content management system (CMS). We are also going to use webhooks for automatic adding, editing, and deleting of items from the Contentful CMS.

CHAPTER 1

Setting up the Ecommerce Site

In this chapter we will cover how to create a new project, then manage default files, and finally install react-icons into the project.

Getting Started

We first need to create a new project with the familiar `gatsby new <project_name>` command. I used the command in my Desktop with the command `gatsby new restaurant-gatsby`.

Next, let's navigate to the directory and open the project in VS Code (Figure 1-1).

Figure 1-1. *cd and code*

It is showing perfectly at `http://localhost:8000/` with the starter project (Figure 1-2).

3

© Nabendu Biswas 2021
N. Biswas, *Advanced Gatsby Projects*, https://doi.org/10.1007/978-1-4842-6640-3_1

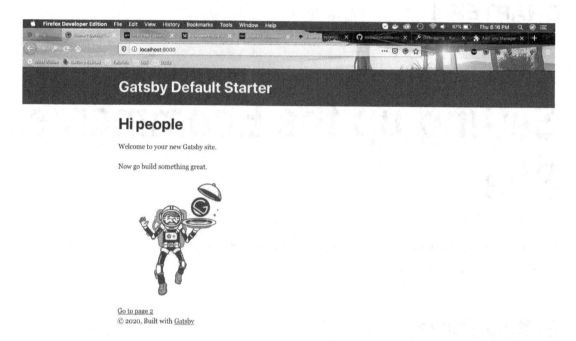

Figure 1-2. *Gatsby starter*

Managing the Default Files

It's time to update and delete some default files. First open the `gatsby-config.js` file and change the content as shown in bold in Listing 1-1.

Listing 1-1. `gatsby-config.js`

```
module.exports = {
  siteMetadata: {
    title: `Restaurant Site`,
    description: `The Restaurant Site`,
    author: `@thewebdev`,
  },
...
...
```

Next, remove `page-2.js` inside the pages folder. Also, update `layout.js` to contain the minimum code for now, as shown in Listing 1-2.

Listing 1-2. `layout.js`

```
import React from "react"
import PropTypes from "prop-types"
import "./layout.css"

const Layout = ({ children }) => {
  return (

      <main>{children}</main>

  )
}

Layout.propTypes = {
  children: PropTypes.node.isRequired,
}

export default Layout
```

Next, open the `index.js` file and put code shown in Listing 1-3 in it, after removing everything else.

Listing 1-3. `index.js`

```
import React from "react"
import Layout from "../components/layout"
import SEO from "../components/seo"

const IndexPage = () => (
  <Layout>
    <SEO title="Home" />
    <h3>The Restaurant Site</h3>
  </Layout>
)

export default IndexPage
```

Delete everything inside `layout.css`, and replace it with the content given in Listing 1-4.

Listing 1-4. `layout.css`

```css
* {
  margin: 0;
  padding: 0;
  box-sizing: border-box;
}

body{
  font-family: 'Caveat', cursive;
}
```

Now, we are mainly going to use styled components in our project. As per the documentation provided at https://www.gatsbyjs.org/packages/gatsby-plugin-styled-components/?=styled, we need to do npm install first.

npm install --save gatsby-plugin-styled-components styled-components babel-plugin-styled-components

So, stop gatsby develop and install the plug-in. Now, we have to open gatsby-config.js and add the lines shown in bold in Listing 1-5.

Listing 1-5. `gatsby-config.js`

```js
module.exports = {
  siteMetadata: {
    title: `Restaurant Site`,
    description: `The Restaurant Site`,
    author: `@thewebdev`,
  },
  plugins: [
    ...
    ...
    `gatsby-plugin-sharp`,
    {
      resolve: `gatsby-plugin-styled-components`,
      options: {
        // Add any options here
      },
```

```
    },
    {
      resolve: `gatsby-plugin-manifest`,
      options: {
        name: `gatsby-starter-default`,
        short_name: `starter`,
        start_url: `/`,
        background_color: `#663399`,
        theme_color: `#663399`,
        display: `minimal-ui`,
        icon: `src/images/gatsby-icon.png`, // This path is relative to the
                                            root of the site.
      },
    },
  ],
}
```

Now, we will use this styled component in our project. Head over to layout.js and update it as follows. We have first removed the import to layout.css and added a GlobalStyle component. We need to import it from styled-components. The updated code is shown in bold in Listing 1-6.

Listing 1-6. layout.js

```
import React from "react"
import PropTypes from "prop-types"
import { createGlobalStyle } from 'styled-components'

const Layout = ({ children }) => {
  return (

      <GlobalStyle />
      <main>{children}</main>

  )
}
```

```
const GlobalStyle = createGlobalStyle`
* {
  margin: 0;
  padding: 0;
  box-sizing: border-box;
}
body {
  font-family: 'Open Sans', sans-serif;
  color:#262626;
  background:#fff;
}
`

Layout.propTypes = {
  children: PropTypes.node.isRequired,
}

export default Layout
```

Now, start `gatsby develop`. The site will look like Figure 1-3.

Figure 1-3. *localhost*

Next, we will install `react-icons` (see `https://www.npmjs.com/package/react-icons`) in the project.

Installing `react-icons`

To install `react-icons` we must stop `gatsby develop` and then enter the command `npm install --save react-icons`.

Navigate to `index.js` and update the code as shown next, to include an icon for black tie. The updated code is shown in bold in Listing 1-7.

Listing 1-7. `index.js`

```
import React from "react"
import Layout from "../components/layout"
import { FaBlackTie } from "react-icons/fa"
import SEO from "../components/seo"

const IndexPage = () => (
  <Layout>
    <SEO title="Home" />
    <h3><FaBlackTie />The Restaurant Site</h3>
  </Layout>
)

export default IndexPage
```

It is displayed perfectly in localhost (Figure 1-4).

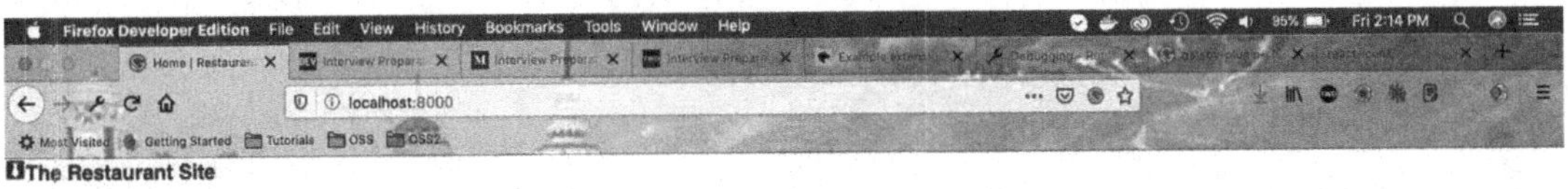

Figure 1-4. *localhost*

Our setup is complete.

Summary

In this chapter, we learned to create a new Gatsby project, then manage default files, and finally install `react-icons` into the project.

In the next chapter, we will start creating real parts of the project.

CHAPTER 2

Adding Core Features to the Ecommerce Site

In this chapter we are going to create most of our Gatsby site, which includes the Navbar, the images, banner text, buttons, and the footer section. We are also going to deploy it to Netlify and show a nice Gallery section.

Navbar

We will start by creating the Navbar.

Basic Setup

Create a folder `globals` inside the `components` folder, and then add a `navbar` folder in it. Then create four files inside the `navbar` folder: `Navbar.js`, `NavbarIcons.js`, `NavbarLinks.js`, and `NavbarHeader.js`.

Put the content shown in Listing 2-1 in the `Navbar.js` file.

Listing 2-1. New file `Navbar.js`

```
import React, { Component } from 'react'
import NavbarHeader from './NavbarHeader'
import NavbarLinks from './NavbarLinks'
import NavbarIcons from './NavbarIcons'

class Navbar extends Component {
  render() {
    return (
```

© Nabendu Biswas 2021
N. Biswas, *Advanced Gatsby Projects*, https://doi.org/10.1007/978-1-4842-6640-3_2

```
      <nav>
        <NavbarHeader />
        <NavbarLinks />
        <NavbarIcons />
      </nav>
    )
  }
}

export default Navbar
```

Next, add the following content in the `NavbarIcons.js` file. We are adding only the basic content now, as in shown in Listing 2-2.

Listing 2-2. New file `NavbarIcons.js`

```
import React, { Component } from 'react'

class NavbarIcons extends Component {
  render() {
    return (
      <div>
        component NavbarIcons
      </div>
    )
  }
}

export default NavbarIcons
```

Next, add the content shown in Listing 2-3 in the `NavbarLinks.js` file.

Listing 2-3. New file `NavbarLinks.js`

```
import React, { Component } from 'react'

class NavbarLinks extends Component {
  render() {
    return (
```

```
    <div>
      component NavbarLinks
    </div>
  )
  }
}

export default NavbarLinks
```

Next, put the content shown in Listing 2-4 into the NavbarHeader.js file.

Listing 2-4. New file NavbarHeader.js

```
import React, { Component } from 'react'

class NavbarHeader extends Component {
  render() {
    return (
      <div>
        component NavbarHeader
      </div>
    )
  }
}

export default NavbarHeader
```

Now, because all the components are created, we will see the Navbar in the layout.js file. The updated code is shown in bold in Listing 2-5.

Listing 2-5. Updating layout.js to show Navbar

```
import React from "react"
import PropTypes from "prop-types"
import { createGlobalStyle } from 'styled-components'
import Navbar from "./globals/navbar/Navbar"

const Layout = ({ children }) => {
  return (
```

```
        <GlobalStyle />
        <Navbar />
        <main>{children}</main>

    )
}

...

...
```

Our Navbar is showing perfectly in localhost (Figure 2-1).

Figure 2-1. *localhost*

Next, we will add `NavWrapper` styles for smaller screens in the `Navbar.js` file, by using `styled-components`.

We are also creating a state variable `navbarOpen`, which we are passing as props to the `NavbarLinks` component. We are also creating a function `handleNavbar()`, which has been used to set the state. We are passing it to the `NavbarHeader` component. The updated code is shown in bold in Listing 2-6.

Listing 2-6. Adding styles and state in `Navbar.js`

```
...
import NavbarIcons from './NavbarIcons'
import styled from 'styled-components'

class Navbar extends Component {
  state = {
    navbarOpen: false,
  }
```

```
handleNavbar = () => {
    this.setState({
        navbarOpen: !this.state.navbarOpen
    })
}

render() {
  return (
    <NavWrapper>
      <NavbarHeader handleNavbar={() => this.handleNavbar} />
      <NavbarLinks navbarOpen={this.state.navbarOpen} />
      <NavbarIcons />
    </NavWrapper>
  )
}
}

const NavWrapper = styled.nav`
    @media (min-width: 768px) {
        display: flex;
        align-items: center;
    }
`

export default Navbar
```

I have also added new pictures to the project in the images folder (Figure 2-2). You can take them from the GitHub link at the end of the post.

Figure 2-2. *Images*

NavbarHeader Component

Next, let's complete our NavbarHeader component. Navigate to the NavbarHeader.js file and update the code as shown in Listing 2-7.

Here, we are getting the props handleNavbar and passing it as a callback function when we click on the FaAlignRight icon.

We have also added a styled component HeaderWrapper and inside it given styles for toggle-icon. Notice that we are not displaying the toggle-icon on larger screens.

Listing 2-7. Updating NavbarHeader.js

```
import React from 'react'
import { Link } from 'gatsby'
import logo from '../../../images/logo.svg'
import { FaAlignRight } from 'react-icons/fa'
import styled from 'styled-components'
```

```
export default function NavbarHeader({ handleNavbar }) {
    return (
        <HeaderWrapper>
            <Link to="/">
                <img src={logo} alt="company logo" />
            </Link>
        <FaAlignRight className="toggle-icon" onClick={() =>
        {handleNavbar()}} />
        </HeaderWrapper>
    )
}

const HeaderWrapper = styled.div`
    padding: 0.4rem 1rem;
    display: flex;
    align-items: center;
    justify-content: space-between;
    .toggle-icon {
        font-size: 1.75rem;
        cursor: pointer;
    }
    @media (min-width: 768px) {
        .toggle-icon {
            display: none;
        }
        padding: 0.4rem 1rem;
    }
```

Now, our site looks like Figure 2-3 on larger screens.

Figure 2-3. *Larger screens*

Figure 2-4 shows how it will display on smaller screens. Notice that the toggle icon is displayed on this screen.

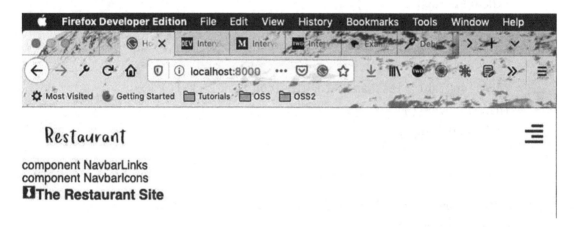

Figure 2-4. *Smaller screens*

We will start creating generic styled components here so that we don't have to create different styles in each project. These styles are also reusable in other parts of the project.

Create a folder named `utils` inside the `src` folder. Create a file named `styles.js` inside the `utils` folder and add the content from Listing 2-8 in the file.

Listing 2-8. New file `styles.js`

```
export const colors = {
  mainWhite: `#fff`,
  mainBlack: `#262626`,
  mainYellow: `#d2aa5c`,
  mainYellow2: `#F2AF29`,
  mainGrey: `#474747`,
}
```

We will soon have other files inside the `utils` folder. Create a root file `index.js` inside it and add the content shown in Listing 2-9 in it.

Listing 2-9. New file `index.js` inside `utils` folder

```
import * as styles from './styles'

export { styles }
```

Let's now use the styles in the `NavbarHeader.js` file. The updated code is shown in bold in Listing 2-10.

Listing 2-10. Using new styles in `NavbarHeader.js`

```
...
import styled from 'styled-components'
import { styles } from '../../../utils'

export default function NavbarHeader({ handleNavbar }) {
    return (
        <HeaderWrapper>
        ...
        ...
        </HeaderWrapper>
    )
}

const HeaderWrapper = styled.div`
    padding: 0.4rem 1rem;
    display: flex;
    align-items: center;
    justify-content: space-between;
    .toggle-icon {
        font-size: 1.75rem;
        color: ${styles.colors.mainYellow};
        cursor: pointer;
    }
    @media (min-width: 768px) {
        .toggle-icon {
            display: none;
        }
        padding: 0.4rem 1rem;
    }
`
```

Now, the Toggle bar shows the mobile menu in yellow (Figure 2-5).

Figure 2-5. *Toggle bar*

NavbarLinks Component

Next, we will start working on the NavbarLinks.js file. We will first add some more imports and a new state variable in the file.

Next, we will render this state variable links by using a map. We are also using the props navbarOpen in the styled component LinkWrapper. The code for these is shown in Listing 2-11.

Listing 2-11. Adding state and rendering it in NavbarLinks.js

```
import React, { Component } from 'react'
import styled from 'styled-components'
import { Link } from 'gatsby'
import { styles } from '../../../utils'

class NavbarLinks extends Component {
    state = {
        links: [
            {
                id: 0,
                path: '/',
                name: 'home',
            },
```

```
            {
                id: 1,
                path: '/about/',
                name: 'about',
            },
            {
                id: 2,
                path: '/menu/',
                name: 'menu',
            },
            {
              id: 3,
              path: '/contact/',
              name: 'contact',
            },
        ],
    }

    render() {
        return (
            <LinkWrapper open={this.props.navbarOpen}>
                {this.state.links.map(item => {
                    return (
                        <li key={item.id}>
                            <Link to={item.path} className="nav-link">
                                {item.name}
                            </Link>
                        </li>
                    )
                })}
            </LinkWrapper>
        )
    }
}
```

```
const LinkWrapper = styled.ul`
`;

export default NavbarLinks
```

It will show our new links on smaller screens (see Figure 2-6), but we need to style them.

Figure 2-6. *Links displayed on a smaller screen*

We will add simple styles for the menu including hover style in the styled component `LinkWrapper` as shown in Listing 2-12.

Listing 2-12. Styles for menu in `NavbarLinks.js`

```
const LinkWrapper = styled.ul`
  li {
    list-style-type: none;
  }
  .nav-link {
    display: block;
    text-decoration: none;
    padding: 0.5rem 1rem 0.5rem 1rem;
    color: ${styles.colors.mainGrey};
    font-weight: 700;
    text-transform: capitalize;
    cursor: pointer;
    ${styles.transDefault};
    &:hover {
        background: ${styles.colors.mainGrey};
        color: ${styles.colors.mainYellow};
```

```
        padding: 0.5rem 1rem 0.5rem 1.3rem;
    }
  }
`;
```

We also need to add a new style for transitions in the styles.js file. The updated code is shown in bold in Listing 2-13.

Listing 2-13. New styles for transitions in styles.js

```
export const colors = {
  mainWhite: `#fff`,
  mainBlack: `#262626`,
  mainYellow: `#d2aa5c`,
  mainYellow2: `#F2AF29`,
  mainGrey: `#474747`,
}
export const transDefault = 'transition:all 0.5s ease-in-out';
```

It shows our menu correctly with a hover effect (Figure 2-7).

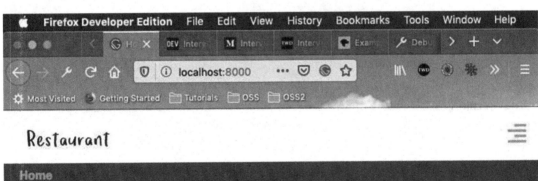

Figure 2-7. *Hover effect*

We will now add the logic to toggle the menu on a smaller screen. We will be using the open for this, which we are passing to the `LinkWrapper` styled component. The props navbarOpen is initially false and will change to true once we click the Menu button. The updated code is shown in bold in Listing 2-14.

Listing 2-14. Toggle menu code in `NavbarLinks.js`

```
...
...
render() {
        return (
            <LinkWrapper open={this.props.navbarOpen}>
                {this.state.links.map(item => {
                ...
                ...
                })}
            </LinkWrapper>
        )
    }
}
const LinkWrapper = styled.ul`
  li {
    list-style-type: none;
  }
  .nav-link {
    ...
    ...
    &:hover {
        background: ${styles.colors.mainGrey};
        color: ${styles.colors.mainYellow};
        padding: 0.5rem 1rem 0.5rem 1.3rem;
    }
  }
```

```
  height: ${props => (props.open ? '152px' : '0px')};
  overflow: hidden;
`;
```

```
export default NavbarLinks
```

We also made one mistake in the parent Navbar.js file. The changes, which we had made, are shown in bold in Listing 2-15.

Listing 2-15. Rectifying mistake in Navbar.js

```
class Navbar extends Component {
  state = {
    navbarOpen: false,
  }

  handleNavbar = () => {
    this.setState(() => {
      return { navbarOpen: !this.state.navbarOpen }
    })
  }
  render() {
    return (
      <NavWrapper>
        <NavbarHeader handleNavbar={this.handleNavbar} />
        <NavbarLinks navbarOpen={this.state.navbarOpen} />
        <NavbarIcons />
      </NavWrapper>
    )
  }
}
```

The code is now working perfectly in localhost when the Menu button is clicked (Figure 2-8).

Figure 2-8. *Gif*

You can find the code for this project in the GitHub repo at `https://github.com/nabendu82/restaurant-gatsby`. We will continue working on the Navbar in this part, first by adding a transition to the `styles.js` file.

We are using es6 default parameters here, so if we pass an empty object we will get these default values. The updated code is shown in bold in Listing 2-16.

Listing 2-16. Adding `transObject` in `styles.js`

```
export const colors = {
  mainWhite: `#fff`,
  mainBlack: `#262626`,
  mainYellow: `#d2aa5c`,
  mainYellow2: `#F2AF29`,
  mainGrey: `#474747`,
}

export const transDefault = 'transition:all 0.5s ease-in-out';

export const transObject = ({ property = 'all', time = '0.5s', type =
'ease-in-out' }) => {
  return `transition:${property} ${time} ${type}`
}
```

Next, let's use it in the `NavbarLinks.js` file. We are changing the `time` to `1s`, and the property and the type fields will be taken from the default parameters. The updated code is shown in bold in Listing 2-17.

Listing 2-17. Using new `transObject` in `NavbarLinks.js`

```
const LinkWrapper = styled.ul`
  li {
    list-style-type: none;
  }
  .nav-link {
  ...
  ...
  }
  height: ${props => (props.open ? '152px' : '0px')};
  overflow: hidden;
  ${styles.transObject({ time: '1s' })};
`;

export default NavbarLinks
```

We need to add the styles for the Navbar for bigger screens, so we will add media queries for it. The updated code is shown in bold in Listing 2-18.

Listing 2-18. Styling Navbar for bigger screens in `NavbarLinks.js`

```
const LinkWrapper = styled.ul`
  li {
    list-style-type: none;
  }
  .nav-link {
  ...
  ...
  }
  height: ${props => (props.open ? '152px' : '0px')};
  overflow: hidden;
  ${styles.transObject({ time: '1s' })};
  @media (min-width: 768px) {
    height: auto;
    display: flex;
    margin: 0 auto;
        .nav-link:hover {
            background: ${styles.colors.mainWhite};
            padding: 0.5rem 1rem 0.5rem 1rem;
        }
  }
`;

export default NavbarLinks
```

Now, our Navbar displays perfectly on bigger screens (Figure 2-9).

Figure 2-9. *Navbar*

NavbarIcons Component

Next, we will start with our `NavbarIcons` component, where we will add our social media links. Open your `NavbarIcons.js` file and make the updates that follow.

Here, we are using code similar to that used for the `NavbarLinks` component. We will first import some `react-icons` and styled components. Then we create a state object with three social media icons. After that, we loop through the icons and render it.

Next, we will add styles for these icons. We are not going to show these icons on small screens, so we will make `display: none` for it. The code for this is given in Listing 2-19.

Listing 2-19. Updating `NavbarIcons.js`

```
import React, { Component } from 'react'
import { FaInstagram, FaTwitter, FaFacebook } from 'react-icons/fa'
import styled from 'styled-components'
import { styles } from '../../../utils'

class NavbarIcons extends Component {
    state = {
        icons: [
            { id: 1, icon: <FaFacebook className="icon facebook-icon" />,
            path: `https://www.facebook.com` },
            { id: 2, icon: <FaTwitter className="icon twitter-icon" />,
            path: `https://www.facebook.com` },
            { id: 3, icon: <FaInstagram className="icon instagram-icon" />,
            path: `https://www.facebook.com` }
        ],
    }
    render() {
        return (
            <IconWrapper>
                {this.state.icons.map(item => (
                    <a href={item.path} key={item.id} target="_blank"
                    rel="noopener noreferrer">
                        {item.icon}
                    </a>
```

```
                ))}
            </IconWrapper>
        )
    }
}

const IconWrapper = styled.div`
    .icon {
        font-size: 1.3rem;
        cursor: pointer;
        ${styles.transObject({})};
    }
    .facebook-icon {
        color: #3b579d;
    }
    .twitter-icon {
        color: #3ab7f0;
    }
    .instagram-icon {
        color: #da5f53;
    }
    .icon:hover {
        color: ${styles.colors.mainYellow};
    }
    display: none;
    @media (min-width: 768px) {
        width: 8rem;
        display: flex;
        justify-content: space-around;
    }
`;

export default NavbarIcons
```

Now, our project will look like Figure 2-10 on larger screens.

Figure 2-10. *Larger screen display*

Those icons will not be shown on smaller screens (Figure 2-11).

Figure 2-11. *Smaller screens*

Let's create the pages for these new links. We will create basic content now and then to create the whole component later.

First create the file about.js in the pages folder and include the basic content shown in Listing 2-20 in it.

Listing 2-20. New file about.js

```
import React from "react"
import Layout from "../components/layout"
import SEO from "../components/seo"
```

```
const AboutPage = () => {
  return (
    <Layout>
      <SEO title="About" />
      <h3>About Page</h3>
    </Layout>
  )
}
```

```
export default AboutPage
```

Next, create a file named `contact.js` inside the pages folder and inclue the content in Listing 2-21 in it.

Listing 2-21. New file `contact.js`

```
import React from 'react'
import Layout from "../components/layout"
import SEO from "../components/seo"
```

```
const ContactPage = () => {
  return (
    <Layout>
      <SEO title="Contact" />
      <h3>Contact Page</h3>
    </Layout>
  )
}
```

```
export default ContactPage
```

Next, create a file named `menu.js` inside the pages folder. Include the content shown in Listing 2-22 in the file.

Listing 2-22. New file `menu.js`

```
import React from 'react'
import Layout from "../components/layout"
import SEO from "../components/seo"
```

```
const MenuPage = () => {
  return (
    <Layout>
      <SEO title="Menu" />
      <h3>Menu Page</h3>
    </Layout>
  )
}

export default MenuPage
```

After checking, all four pages should be working perfectly (Figure 2-12).

Figure 2-12. *Contact page*

Displaying a Center Image

We will next start to work on displaying a center image on the home page. First add a new file Header.js inside the utils folder and include the content shown in Listing 2-23 in the file.

We are taking img and children as props and showing a styled-component IndexHeader. We are also importing the img and using it as default props at Line 18, which will allow you to show the image even if it is not supplied by the parent component.

Listing 2-23. New file Header.js

```
import styled from 'styled-components'
import React from 'react'
import img from '../images/bcg/homeBcg.jpg'

function HomeHeader({ img, children }) {
    return <IndexHeader img={img}>{children}</IndexHeader>
}
```

```
const IndexHeader = styled.header`
    min-height: calc(100vh - 68px);
    background: linear-gradient(rgba(0, 0, 0, 0.4), rgba(0, 0, 0, 0.4)),
        url(${props => props.img}) center/cover fixed no-repeat;
    display: flex;
    justify-content: center;
    align-items: center;
`

HomeHeader.defaultProps = {
    img: img,
}

export { HomeHeader }
```

Next, let's add this HomeHeader to the index.js file inside the utils folder. The updated content is shown in bold in Listing 2-24.

Listing 2-24. Exporting HomeHeader from index.js, inside the utils folder

```
import * as styles from './styles'
import { HomeHeader } from './Header'

export { HomeHeader, styles }
```

Now, we will use this in our index.js file inside the pages folder, to display it on the home screen. The updated content is shown in bold in Listing 2-25.

Listing 2-25. Adding HomeHeader in index.js inside the pages folder

```
import React from "react"
import Layout from "../components/layout"
import { HomeHeader } from "../utils"
import img from '../images/bcg/homeBcg.jpg'
import SEO from "../components/seo"

const IndexPage = () => (
  <Layout>
    <SEO title="Home" />
    <HomeHeader img={img}>
```

```
    <h3>The Restaurant Site</h3>
  </HomeHeader>
 </Layout>
)

export default IndexPage
```

This displays the image on our home page, as shown in Figure 2-13.

Figure 2-13. *Image displayed on the home page*

Now, we will add the logic for other pages. Navigate to the Header.js file and add the changes shown in bold in Listing 2-26. We are adding a new component PageHeader, which is similar to HomeHeader but uses a different styled-component , DefaultHeader.

The styled-component DefaultHeader uses all the styles from IndexHeader except the minimum height.

After that, we are add PageHeader in default props and export. The updated content is shown in bold in Listing 2-26.

Listing 2-26. Adding PageHeader component in Header.js

```
...
...

function HomeHeader({ img, children }) {
    return <IndexHeader img={img}>{children}</IndexHeader>
}

function PageHeader({ img, children }) {
    return <DefaultHeader img={img}>{children}</DefaultHeader>
}

const IndexHeader = styled.header`
...
...
`

const DefaultHeader = styled(IndexHeader)`
    min-height: 60vh;
`

HomeHeader.defaultProps = {
    img: img,
}

PageHeader.defaultProps = {
    img: img,
}

export { HomeHeader, PageHeader }
```

After that we add the PageHeader in the index.js file inside the utils folder. The updated content is shown in bold in Listing 2-27.

Listing 2-27. Export PageHeader from index.js

```
import * as styles from './styles'
import { HomeHeader, PageHeader } from './Header'

export { HomeHeader, PageHeader, styles }
```

Next, let's use the PageHeader in the about.js file inside the pages folder. The updated content is shown in bold in Listing 2-28.

Listing 2-28. Using PageHeader in about.js

```
import React from "react"
import Layout from "../components/layout"
import SEO from "../components/seo"
import { PageHeader } from "../utils"
import aboutImg from '../images/bcg/aboutBcg.jpg'

const AboutPage = () => {
  return (
    <Layout>
      <SEO title="About" />
      <PageHeader img={aboutImg}>
        <h3>About Page</h3>
      </PageHeader>
    </Layout>
  )
}

export default AboutPage
```

Now, our About page will show the image shown in Figure 2-14.

Figure 2-14. *About page*

Next, let's use the PageHeader in the contact.js file inside the pages folder. The updated content is shown in bold in Listing 2-29.

Listing 2-29. Using PageHeader in contact.js

```
import React from 'react'
import Layout from "../components/layout"
import SEO from "../components/seo"
import { PageHeader } from "../utils"
import contactImg from '../images/bcg/contactBcg.jpg'

const ContactPage = () => {
  return (
    <Layout>
      <SEO title="Contact" />
      <PageHeader img={contactImg}>
        <h3>Contact Page</h3>
      </PageHeader>
```

```
    </Layout>
  )
}
```

```
export default ContactPage
```

Now, our Contact page will display the contact image, as shown in Figure 2-15.

Figure 2-15. *Contact page*

Next, let's use the PageHeader in the menu.js file inside the pages folder. The updated content is shown in bold in Listing 2-30.

Listing 2-30. Using PageHeader in menu.js

```
import React from 'react'
import Layout from "../components/layout"
import SEO from "../components/seo"
import { PageHeader } from "../utils"
import menuImg from '../images/bcg/menuBcg.jpg'
```

```
const MenuPage = () => {
  return (
    <Layout>
      <SEO title="Menu" />
      <PageHeader img={menuImg}>
        <h3>Menu Page</h3>
      </PageHeader>
    </Layout>
  )
}

export default MenuPage
```

Our Menu page will show the menu image, as displayed in Figure 2-16.

Figure 2-16. *Menu page*

Banner Text and Button

In this section we will create components for banners and buttons. We are going to show these banners inside each image and will use buttons in multiple places.

Banner Component

We will now start creating banner components. This component will show the different text that is displayed inside each picture for each page.

Create a new file named `Banner.js` inside the `utils` folder and include the code shown in Listing 2-31 in the file. This component is quite similar to the `Header` component we created previously. We are taking three props—`title`, `subtitle`, and `children`—and displaying them in a `styled-component` `BannerWrapper`.

We are also using a default props for `title`, if not passed from the parent component. The content this file is given in Listing 2-31.

Listing 2-31. New file `Banner.js`

```
import React from 'react'
import styled from 'styled-components'
import { styles } from '../utils'
export const Banner = ({ title, subtitle, children }) => {
    return (
        <BannerWrapper>
            <h1>{title}</h1>
            <h3>{subtitle}</h3>
            {children}
        </BannerWrapper>
    )
}
const BannerWrapper = styled.div`
    margin-bottom: 3rem;
    text-align: center;
    h1 {
        color: ${styles.colors.mainWhite};
        font-size: 3rem;
```

```
        text-transform: uppercase;
        ${styles.letterSpacing({ spacing: '0.75rem' })};
    }
    h3 {
        color: ${styles.colors.mainWhite};
        ${styles.textSlanted};
        ${styles.letterSpacing({ spacing: '0.15rem' })};
        font-size: 1.5rem;
        text-transform: capitalize;
    }
`

Banner.defaultProps = {
    title: 'default title',
}
```

We are using some additional styles in this Banner.js file, so let's create them in a styles.js file in the same folder. The updated content is shown in bold in Listing 2-32.

Listing 2-32. textSlated and letterSpacing styles in styles.js

```
export const colors = {
...
...
}

export const transDefault = 'transition:all 0.5s ease-in-out';

export const transObject = ({ property = 'all', time = '0.5s', type =
'ease-in-out' }) => {
  return `transition:${property} ${time} ${type}`
}

export const textSlanted = `font-family:'Caveat', cursive;`

export const letterSpacing = ({ spacing = '0.1rem' }) => {
    return `letter-spacing:${spacing}`
}
```

Next, let's add this `Banner` to the `index.js` file inside the `utils` folder. The updated content is shown in bold in Listing 2-33.

Listing 2-33. Adding Banner component in `index.js`

```
import * as styles from './styles'
import { HomeHeader, PageHeader } from './Header'
import { Banner } from './Banner'

export { Banner, HomeHeader, PageHeader, styles }
```

Now, we will use this in our `index.js` file inside the `pages` folder to display it on the home screen. The updated content is shown in bold in Listing 2-34.

Listing 2-34. Using Banner in `index.js`

```
import React from "react"
import Layout from "../components/layout"
import { HomeHeader, Banner } from "../utils"
import img from '../images/bcg/homeBcg.jpg'
import SEO from "../components/seo"

const IndexPage = () => (
  <Layout>
    <SEO title="Home" />
    <HomeHeader img={img}>
      <Banner title="Fine Dining" subtitle="65, MG Road- Bangalore, KA">
      </Banner>
    </HomeHeader>
  </Layout>
)

export default IndexPage
```

Now, the banner is showing perfectly on our home page, inside the photo (Figure 2-17).

Figure 2-17. *Banner appearance on the home page*

Next, let's use the Banner in the about.js file inside the pages folder. The updated content is shown in bold in Listing 2-35.

Listing 2-35. Using Banner in about.js

```
import React from "react"
import Layout from "../components/layout"
import SEO from "../components/seo"
import { PageHeader, Banner } from "../utils"
import aboutImg from '../images/bcg/aboutBcg.jpg'

const AboutPage = () => {
  return (
    <Layout>
      <SEO title="About" />
      <PageHeader img={aboutImg}>
        <Banner title="about us" subtitle="a little about us" />
      </PageHeader>
```

```
      </Layout>
   )
}
```

```
export default AboutPage
```

Our About page will show the text we just added (Figure 2-18).

Figure 2-18. *About page with text*

Next, let's use the Banner in the contact.js file inside the pages folder. The updated content is shown in bold in Listing 2-36.

Listing 2-36. Using Banner in contact.js

```
import React from 'react'
import Layout from "../components/layout"
import SEO from "../components/seo"
import { PageHeader, Banner } from "../utils"
import contactImg from '../images/bcg/contactBcg.jpg'
```

```
const ContactPage = () => {
  return (
    <Layout>
      <SEO title="Contact" />
      <PageHeader img={contactImg}>
        <Banner title="contact us" subtitle="let's get in touch" />
      </PageHeader>
    </Layout>
  )
}
```

```
export default ContactPage
```

Our Contact page will now display the contact text (Figure 2-19).

Figure 2-19. *Contact page*

Next, let's use the Banner in the `menu.js` file inside the `pages` folder. The updated content is shown in bold in Listing 2-37.

Listing 2-37. Using Banner in `menu.js`

```
import React from 'react'
import Layout from "../components/layout"
import SEO from "../components/seo"
import { PageHeader, Banner } from "../utils"
import menuImg from '../images/bcg/menuBcg.jpg'

const MenuPage = () => {
  return (
    <Layout>
      <SEO title="Menu" />
      <PageHeader img={menuImg}>
        <Banner title="our menu" subtitle="The best in town" />
      </PageHeader>
    </Layout>
  )
}

export default MenuPage
```

Now, our Menu page will show the menu text added (Figure 2-20).

Figure 2-20. *Menu page*

Button Component

We will start this part by creating the banner button component. This will allow us to place a button within each picture below the banner text.

First, create a new file named Button.js inside the utils folder and include the content given in Listing 2-38 in the file. This is a simple component that has mainly a styled-component BannerButton.

Listing 2-38. New Button.js file

```
import styled from 'styled-components'
import { styles } from '../utils'

const BannerButton = styled.button`
    display: block;
    color: ${styles.colors.mainWhite};
    background: transparent;
    padding: 0.5rem 1rem;
```

```
    text-transform: uppercase;
    font-size: 1.5rem;
    letter-spacing: 0.5rem;
    font-weight: 700;
    ${styles.border({ color: `${styles.colors.mainWhite}` })};
    margin-top: 1rem;
    ${styles.transObject({})};
    &:hover {
        background: ${styles.colors.mainWhite};
        color: ${styles.colors.mainBlack};
        cursor: pointer;
    }
`

export { BannerButton }
```

We are using an additional style border in the this Button.js file, so let's create it in styles.js in the same folder. Add the content in Listing 2-39 at the end of the styles.js file.

Listing 2-39. New border style in styles.js

```
export const border = ({ width = '0.15rem', type = 'solid', color = 'white'
}) => {
    return `border:${width} ${type} ${color}`
}
```

Next, let's add this BannerButton to the index.js file inside the utils folder. The updated content is shown in bold in Listing 2-40.

Listing 2-40. Adding BannerButton in index.js

```
import * as styles from './styles'
import { HomeHeader, PageHeader } from './Header'
import { Banner } from './Banner'
import { BannerButton } from './Button'

export { BannerButton, Banner, HomeHeader, PageHeader, styles }
```

Now, we will use BannerButton in our index.js file inside the pages folder to display it on the home page. Notice that we are using inline styling to center the button. The updated content for the same file is given in Listing 2-41.

Listing 2-41. Adding BannerButton in index.js

```
import React from "react"
import Layout from "../components/layout"
import { HomeHeader, Banner, BannerButton } from "../utils"
import img from '../images/bcg/homeBcg.jpg'
import SEO from "../components/seo"

const IndexPage = () => (
  <Layout>
    <SEO title="Home" />
    <HomeHeader img={img}>
      <Banner title="Fine Dining" subtitle="65, MG Road- Bangalore, KA">
        <BannerButton style={{ margin: '2rem auto' }}>menu</BannerButton>
      </Banner>
    </HomeHeader>
  </Layout>
)

export default IndexPage
```

Now, the banner button is displayed perfectly on our home page, inside the photo and below the banner text (Figure 2-21).

Figure 2-21. *Banner button*

Home Component

We will have different sections on our home page. Let's create a folder named
HomeComponents for it inside the components folder. After that, create a file named
QuickInfo.js inside it and include the content in Listing 2-42 in the file.

Listing 2-42. New file QuickInfo.js

```
import React, { Component } from 'react'
import { Section, Title } from '../../utils'

export default class QuickInfo extends Component {
  render() {
    return (
      <Section>
```

```
        <Title message="let us tell you" title="our misson" />
      </Section>
    )
  }
}
```

Next, we will create the Section component, which we are using in the QuickInfo component. Create a file named Section.js inside the utils folder and add the content given in Listing 2-43 in the file.

Listing 2-43. New utils file Section.js

```
import styled from 'styled-components'

export const Section = styled.section`
    padding: 2rem 0;
    width: 90vw;
    margin: 0 auto;

`
```

Next, create a file named Title.js inside the utils folder and put the content given in Listing 2-44 in the file. We are taking the props message and title and styling them through a styled-component TitleWrapper.

Listing 2-44. New file Title.js

```
import React from 'react'
import styled from 'styled-components'
import { styles } from '.'

export function Title({ title, message }) {
    return (
        <TitleWrapper>
            <h3>{message}</h3>
            <h1>{title}</h1>
            <div className="underline" />
        </TitleWrapper>
    )
}
```

```
Title.defaultProps = { message: 'our message', title: 'our title' }

const TitleWrapper = styled.div`
  text-align: center;
  h3 {
    ${styles.textSlanted};
    ${styles.letterSpacing({ spacing: '0.3rem' })};
    font-size: 2rem;
    color: ${styles.colors.mainYellow};
  }
  h1 {
    ${styles.letterSpacing({ spacing: '0.3rem' })};
    font-size: 2rem;
    text-transform: uppercase;
  }
  .underline {
    width: 5rem;
    height: 0.2rem;
    background: ${styles.colors.mainYellow};
    margin: 0.5rem auto;
  }`
```

Next, we need to add them in the index.js file in the same utils folder. The updated content is shown in bold in Listing 2-45.

Listing 2-45. Adding section and title in index.js

```
import * as styles from './styles'
import { HomeHeader, PageHeader } from './Header'
import { Banner } from './Banner'
import { BannerButton } from './Button'
import { Section } from './Section'
import { Title } from './Title'

export { Title, Section, BannerButton, Banner, HomeHeader, PageHeader,
styles }
```

Now, we will use QuickInfo in our index.js file inside the pages folder to display it on the home page. The updated content is shown in bold in Listing 2-46.

Listing 2-46. Using QuickInfo in index.js

```
...
import SEO from "../components/seo"
import QuickInfo from '../components/HomeComponents/QuickInfo'

const IndexPage = () => (
  <Layout>
    <SEO title="Home" />
    <HomeHeader img={img}>
      <Banner title="Fine Dining" subtitle="65, MG Road- Bangalore, KA">
        <BannerButton style={{ margin: '2rem auto' }}>menu</BannerButton>
      </Banner>
    </HomeHeader>
    <QuickInfo />
  </Layout>
)

export default IndexPage
```

Now, the QuickInfo is displayed perfectly on our home page below the photo (Figure 2-22).

Figure 2-22. *Home page with quick info*

You can find the code for the project in the GitHub repo at https://github.com/nabendu82/restaurant-gatsby.

We will next create a button for the QuickInfo section. Let's create a new button named SectionButton in the Button.js file in the utils folder. Here, we are reusing some of the styles from BannerButton and overriding some styles. The updated content is shown in bold in Listing 2-47.

Listing 2-47. Adding SectionButton in Button.js

```
import styled from 'styled-components'
import { styles } from '../utils'

const BannerButton = styled.button`
...

...
`
```

```
const SectionButton = styled(BannerButton)`
    color: ${styles.colors.mainBlack};
    ${styles.border({ color: `${styles.colors.mainBlack}` })};
    &:hover {
        background: ${styles.colors.mainBlack};
        color: ${styles.colors.mainYellow};
        cursor: pointer;
    }
`

export { BannerButton, SectionButton }
```

Next, we need to add SectionButton in the index.js file in the same utils folder. The updated content is shown in bold in Listing 2-48.

Listing 2-48. Adding SectionButton in index.js

```
import * as styles from './styles'
import { HomeHeader, PageHeader } from './Header'
import { Banner } from './Banner'
import { BannerButton, SectionButton } from './Button'
import { Section } from './Section'
import { Title } from './Title'

export { SectionButton, Title, Section, BannerButton, Banner, HomeHeader,
PageHeader, styles }
```

Now, we will use SectionButton in our QuickInfo.js file inside the HomeComponents folder to display it on the home page. The updated content is shown in bold in Listing 2-49.

Listing 2-49. Adding SectionButton in QuickInfo.js

```
import React, { Component } from 'react'
import { Section, Title, SectionButton } from '../../utils'

export default class QuickInfo extends Component {
  render() {
    return (
```

```
<Section>
  <Title message="let us tell you" title="our misson" />
  <SectionButton style={{ margin: '2rem auto' }}>about</
  SectionButton>
</Section>
    )
  }
}
```

Now, the SectionButton will be displayed on our home page below the text (Figure 2-23).

Figure 2-23. *About button*

Next, we will create the text for this section. Update the QuickInfo.js file with the code shown in bold in Listing 2-50. We are adding imports for styled-component and the styles and also adding import for the Link. After that we are wrapping the text and the button created earlier in a new styled-component QuickInfoWrapper.

Next, we will create styles for the QuickInfoWrapper component. We have also created media queries for 768px and 992px.

Listing 2-50. Updating QuickInfo.js

```
import React, { Component } from 'react'
import { Section, Title, SectionButton } from '../../utils'
import styled from 'styled-components'
import { styles } from '../../utils'
import { Link } from 'gatsby'

export default class QuickInfo extends Component {
  render() {
    return (
      <Section>
        <Title message="let us tell you" title="our misson" />
        <QuickInfoWrapper>
          <p className="text">
            Our mission is to serve you authetic dishes from north
            karnataka.
            these dishes are created by our top chefs, from the region.
            Some of our awesome dishes are - Menther kadabu, Pundi Soppu,
            Jolad Rotti, Ragi Ambali, Nargis Man Dak ki, Mudde, Girmit and
            many more.
          </p>
          <Link to="/about/" style={{ textDecoration: "none" }}>
            <SectionButton style={{ margin: "2rem auto" }}>about
            </SectionButton>
          </Link>
        </QuickInfoWrapper>
      </Section>
    )
  }
}

const QuickInfoWrapper = styled.div`
    width: 90%;
```

```
margin: 2rem auto;
.text {
    line-height: 2em;
    color: ${styles.colors.mainGrey};
    word-spacing: 0.2rem;
}

@media (min-width: 768px) {
    width: 70%;
}
@media (min-width: 992px) {
    width: 60%;
}
```

So, at 992px and above it will appear as shown in Figure 2-24.

Figure 2-24. *Display on larger screens*

Between 768px and 992px, it appear as shown in Figure 2-25.

Figure 2-25. *Display on medium-sized screen*

It will appear as shown in Figure 2-26 on mobile screens.

Figure 2-26. *Display on mobile screen*

In the next section we'll create a footer component.

Creating the Footer

We will create a footer now. Create a file named `Footer.js` inside the `globals` folder and include the content from Listing 2-51 in the file.

Here, we are importing `styled-components` and our global style files. After that we are also importing `react-icons` for Facebook, Twitter, and Instagram.

We are creating a state variable icon, containing the three social icons as an array of objects.

We will now show the icons by looping through them and showing an anchor tag for each of them. We have also created a `styled-component FooterWrapper`, and we will complete the styles on `FooterWrapper`.

Listing 2-51. New file `Footer.js`

```
import React, { Component } from 'react'
import styled from 'styled-components'
import { styles } from '../../utils'
import { FaInstagram, FaTwitter, FaFacebook } from 'react-icons/fa'
class Footer extends Component {
    state = {
        icons: [
            {
                id: 1,
                icon: <FaFacebook className="icon facebook-icon" />,
                path: `https://www.facebook.com`,
            },
            {
                id: 2,
                icon: <FaTwitter className="icon twitter-icon" />,
                path: `https://www.twitter.com`,
            },
            {
                id: 3,
                icon: <FaInstagram className="icon instagram-icon" />,
                path: `https://www.instagram.com`,
            },
```

```
        ],
    }
    render() {
        return (
            <FooterWrapper>
                <div className="title">restaurant</div>
                <div className="icons">
                    {this.state.icons.map(item => (
                        <a href={item.path} key={item.id} target="_blank"
                        rel="noopener noreferrer">
                            {item.icon}
                        </a>
                    ))}
                </div>
                <p className="copyright">copyright &copy; 2020 thewebdev</p>
            </FooterWrapper>
        )
    }
}

const FooterWrapper = styled.footer`
    padding: 2rem 0;
    background: ${styles.colors.mainBlack};
    .icons {
        width: 10rem;
        display: flex;
        justify-content: space-between;
        margin: 0 auto;
    }
    .icon {
        color: ${styles.colors.mainWhite};
        font-size: 1.3rem;
        ${styles.transObject({})};
        &:hover { color: ${styles.colors.mainPrimary};  }
    }
```

```
    .copyright {
        color: ${styles.colors.mainWhite};
        text-transform: capitalize;
        text-align: center;
        margin: 1rem 0;
    }
    .title {
        text-align: center;
        width: 12rem;
        color: ${styles.colors.mainYellow};
        text-transform: uppercase;
        padding: 0.3rem 1rem;
        margin: 0 auto 2rem auto;
        font-size: 1.5rem;
        ${styles.border({ color: `${styles.colors.mainYellow}` })}
    }
`

export default Footer;
```

Next, we will show this component in `layout.js`, as we need to show the footer on all pages. The updated content is shown in bold in Listing 2-52.

Listing 2-52. Adding Footer in `layout.js`

```
...
import Navbar from "./globals/navbar/Navbar"
import Footer from '../components/globals/Footer'

const Layout = ({ children }) => {
  return (

      <GlobalStyle />
      <Navbar />
      {children}
      <Footer />

  )
}
```

```
const GlobalStyle = createGlobalStyle`
...
...
`

Layout.propTypes = {
  children: PropTypes.node.isRequired,
}

export default Layout
```

It will display our footer perfectly on our home page (Figure 2-27).

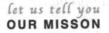

Figure 2-27. *Home page with footer*

Also, because we have put the code in `layout.js`, it is present on other pages, including the About page shown in Figure 2-28.

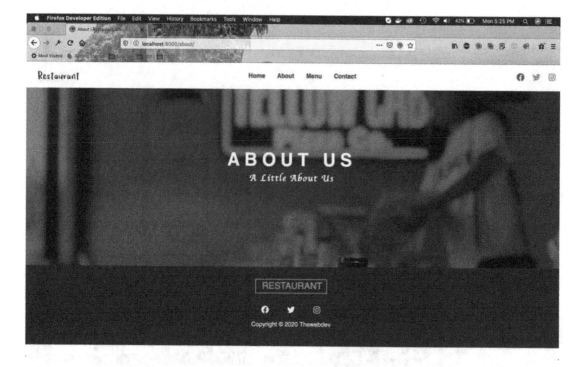

Figure 2-28. *About page with text and footer*

We have completed a large part of the project, so it's time to deploy it in Netlify. I have already pushed all the code up to this part to GitHub.

Deploying in Netlify

In this section, we will deploy our site to Netlify. Once I opened my Netlify dashboard, I was presented with the screen shown in Figure 2-29. Click New site from Git.

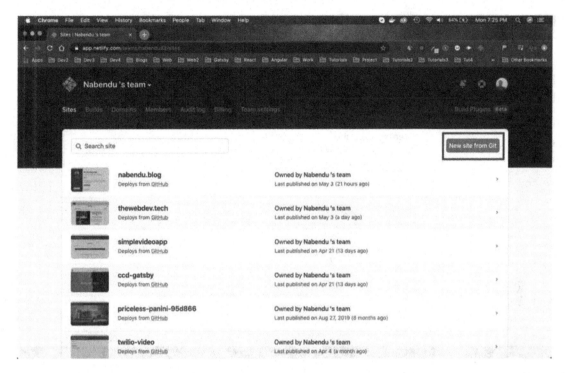

Figure 2-29. *Creating a new site from Git*

On the next screen, click on GitHub, as the code being used is in GitHub (Figure 2-30).

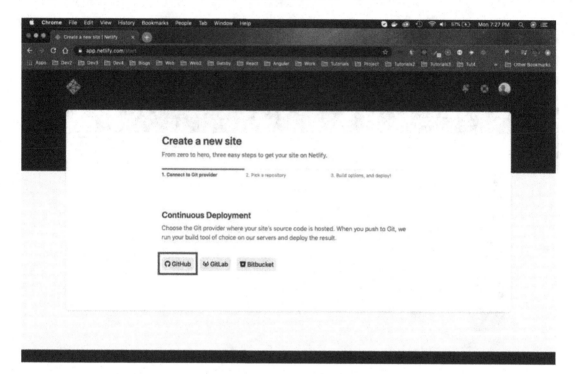

Figure 2-30. *Click GitHub*

Because I had a lot of repos, I needed to search for the repo and click it (Figure 2-31).

Figure 2-31. *Selecting restaurant-gatsby*

On the next screen we need to click Deploy Site (Figure 2-32).

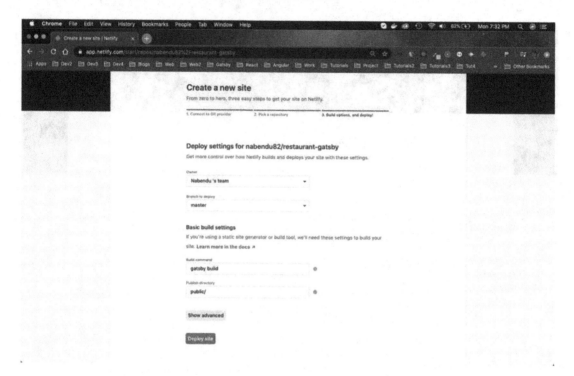

Figure 2-32. *Click Deploy site*

The deployment will begin next and assign a random name to our site. We can change it by clicking Site settings (Figure 2-33).

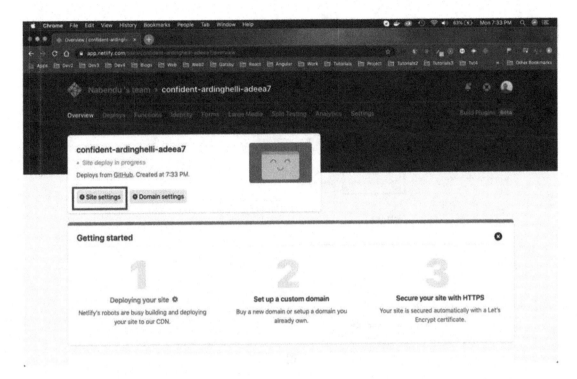

Figure 2-33. *Changing the site name with Site settings*

On the next screen, scroll down and click Change site name (Figure 2-34).

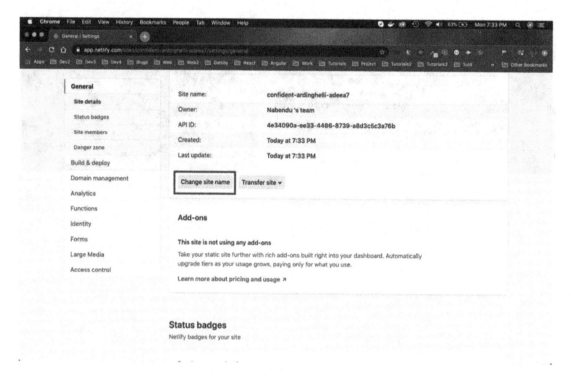

Figure 2-34. *Changing the site name*

That will open a pop-up window in which you can provide the new site name. I tried using `restaurant-gatsby` first, but the name was already taken (Figure 2-35).

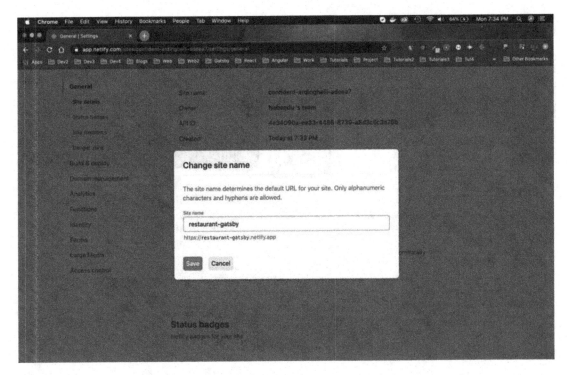

Figure 2-35. `restaurant-gatsby`

After several tries, I settled on `restaurant-bangalore`, as shown in Figure 2-36.

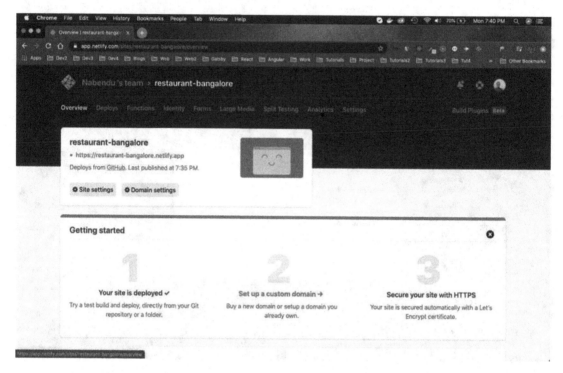

Figure 2-36. `restaurant-bangalore`

The site, shown in Figure 2-37, is live, so we can check it at `https://restaurant-bangalore.netlify.app/`. The live site will auto-deploy every time we push our code to GitHub.

Figure 2-37. *The live site*

Gallery Component

Next, we will start creating the Gallery component on the home page. Create a new file named Gallery.js in the HomeComponents folder and include the content given in Listing 2-53 in the file. We are using graphql and useStaticQuery to show the image stored in the homeGallery folder.

Listing 2-53. New file Gallery.js

```
import React from 'react'
import styled from 'styled-components'
import { useStaticQuery, graphql } from 'gatsby'
import { styles, Section } from '../../utils'
import Img from 'gatsby-image'

const Gallery = () => {
  const data = useStaticQuery(graphql`
    {
```

```
    img1: file(relativePath: { eq: "homeGallery/img-1.jpeg" }) {
        childImageSharp {
            fluid(maxWidth: 500) {
                ...GatsbyImageSharpFluid_tracedSVG
            }
        }
    }
  }
`)

  return <Img fluid={data.img1.childImageSharp.fluid} />
}

export default Gallery
```

Now, let's display this `Gallery` component on the home page, by adding it to the `index.js` file in pages folder. The updated content is shown in bold in Listing 2-54.

Listing 2-54. Adding `Gallery` in `index.js`

```
...
import QuickInfo from '../components/HomeComponents/QuickInfo'
import Gallery from '../components/HomeComponents/Gallery'

const IndexPage = () => (
  <Layout>
    <SEO title="Home" />
    <HomeHeader img={img}>
      <Banner title="Fine Dining" subtitle="65, MG Road- Bangalore, KA">
        <BannerButton style={{ margin: '2rem auto' }}>menu</BannerButton>
      </Banner>
    </HomeHeader>
    <QuickInfo />
    <Gallery />
  </Layout>
)

export default IndexPage
```

Now the image will be shown on our home page (Figure 2-38).

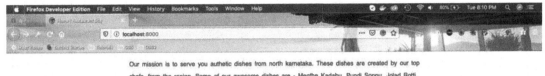

Our mission is to serve you authentic dishes from north karnataka. These dishes are created by our top chefs, from the region. Some of our awesome dishes are - Menthe Kadabu, Pundi Soppu, Jolad Rotti, Ragi Amball, Nargis Man Dak ki, Mudde, Girmit and many more.

ABOUT

Figure 2-38. *Home page with gallery*

Next, we will add two more images in our `Gallery.js` file. For this we will add queries similar to the `img1` query. Next, we will add three constants **img1**, **img2** and **img3** to get these three images.

After that, we will use the `Section` component to wrap everything. Within it, we use the `Gallery-Wrapper styled-component`, in which we are soon going to write code.

After that we use the image and text wrapped within a `div`. The updated content is shown in bold in Listing 2-55.

Listing 2-55. Adding images in `Gallery.js`

```
...

const Gallery = () => {
  const data = useStaticQuery(graphql`
    {
      img1: file(relativePath: { eq: "homeGallery/img-1.jpeg" }) {
        childImageSharp {
          fluid(maxWidth: 500) {
```

```
                    ...GatsbyImageSharpFluid_tracedSVG
              }
          }
      }
    img2: file(relativePath: { eq: "homeGallery/img-2.jpeg" }) {
      childImageSharp {
          fluid(maxWidth: 500) {
              ...GatsbyImageSharpFluid_tracedSVG
          }
        }
      }
    img3: file(relativePath: { eq: "homeGallery/img-3.jpeg" }) {
        childImageSharp {
            fluid(maxWidth: 500) {
                ...GatsbyImageSharpFluid_tracedSVG
            }
          }
      }
  }
`)

const img1 = data.img1.childImageSharp.fluid
const img2 = data.img2.childImageSharp.fluid
const img3 = data.img3.childImageSharp.fluid
return (
    <Section>
        <GalleryWrapper>
            <div className="item item-1">
                <Img fluid={img1} />
                <p className="info">awesome pizza</p>
            </div>
            <div className="item item-2">
                <Img fluid={img2} />
                <p className="info">awesome chicken</p>
            </div>
```

```
        <div className="item item-3">
            <Img fluid={img3} />
            <p className="info">awesome meat</p>
        </div>
    </GalleryWrapper>
  </Section>
 )
}

const GalleryWrapper = styled.div``;

export default Gallery
```

Now all the images and text are shown on our home page (Figure 2-39).

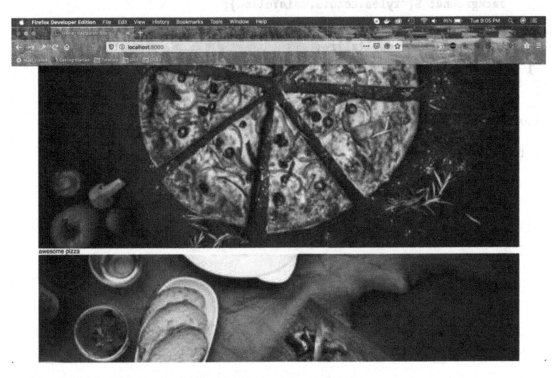

Figure 2-39. *Home page gallery with images and text*

Let's write some styles now. We will first write the styles for mobile screens. The updated content is shown in bold in Listing 2-56.

Listing 2-56. Styles in `Gallery.js`

```
const GalleryWrapper = styled.div`
  display: grid;
  grid-template-columns: auto;
  grid-row-gap: 1rem;
  .item {
      position: relative;
  }
  .info {
      position: absolute;
      top: 0;
      left: 0;
      background: ${styles.colors.mainYellow};
      padding: 0.1rem 0.3rem;
      text-transform: capitalize;
  }
`;

export default Gallery
```

It will now display as shown in Figure 2-40 on mobile screens.

Figure 2-40. *Site on a mobile screen*

Now, we will add styles for two more screen sizes. The updated content is shown in bold in Listing 2-57.

Listing 2-57. Styles for medium screens in `Gallery.js`

```
const GalleryWrapper = styled.div`
  display: grid;
  grid-template-columns: auto;
  grid-row-gap: 1rem;
  .item {
    position: relative;
  }
  .info {
    position: absolute;
    top: 0;
    left: 0;
    background: ${styles.colors.mainYellow};
    padding: 0.1rem 0.3rem;
    text-transform: capitalize;
  }

  @media (min-width: 576px) {
    grid-template-columns: 1fr 1fr;
    grid-column-gap: 1rem;
  }

  @media (min-width: 768px) {
    grid-template-columns: repeat(3, 1fr);
  }
`;

export default Gallery
```

For screen sizes between 576px and 767px, our site will display in a two-column layout (Figure 2-41).

Figure 2-41. *Medium screen display*

For screen sizes between 768px and 991px, our site will display in a three-column layout (Figure 2-42).

Figure 2-42. *Display on a slightly larger screen*

Finally, we will add styles for screen sizes greater and equal to 992px. We are using the concept of `grid-template-areas` here.

Now, we are using a lot of grid concepts in this part. You can learn all about CSS grids from my earlier series at `https://thewebdev.tech/series/Grid-basics`. The updated content is shown in bold in Listing 2-58.

Listing 2-58. Styles for larger screens in `Gallery.js`

```
const GalleryWrapper = styled.div`
  ...
  ...
  @media (min-width: 576px) {
    grid-template-columns: 1fr 1fr;
    grid-column-gap: 1rem;
  }
  @media (min-width: 768px) {
    grid-template-columns: repeat(3, 1fr);
  }
  @media (min-width: 992px) {
    .gatsby-image-wrapper {
        height: 100%;
    }
    grid-template-areas:
        'one one two two'
        'one one three three';
    .item-1 {
        grid-area: one;
    }
    .item-2 {
        grid-area: two;
    }
    .item-3 {
        grid-area: three;
    }
  }
`;

export default Gallery
```

It will display as shown in Figure 2-43 on normal desktop screens.

Figure 2-43. *Display on normal screens*

You can find the code for the project in the GitHub repo at `https://github.com/nabendu82/restaurant-gatsby`.

Summary

In this chapter we created the Navbar, the images, buttons, and a footer section. We also deployed it to Netlify and showed a nice gallery section. In the next chapter, we will learn to store our data in Contentful CMS and fetch data in our application from the CMS.

CHAPTER 3

Setting up Contentful

Contentful is a free-to-use CMS. Every website or mobile app needs to store data and that is done in a database or CMS. The benefit of the Contentful CMS is that it is very easy to edit and generally used by business owners, who don't need to touch the code base.

In this chapter, we create a Contenful account and then a space where we are going to store our data. After that, we will connect it to our app to retrieve the data and display it. We will start with our Contentful CMS setup, from which we will eventually get all our data. Open the Contentful site at `https://www.contentful.com/` and log in.

Creating a Content Model

If you are a first-time user, you will be presented with the screen shown in Figure 3-1. Here you need to click Explore content modeling.

© Nabendu Biswas 2021
N. Biswas, *Advanced Gatsby Projects*, https://doi.org/10.1007/978-1-4842-6640-3_3

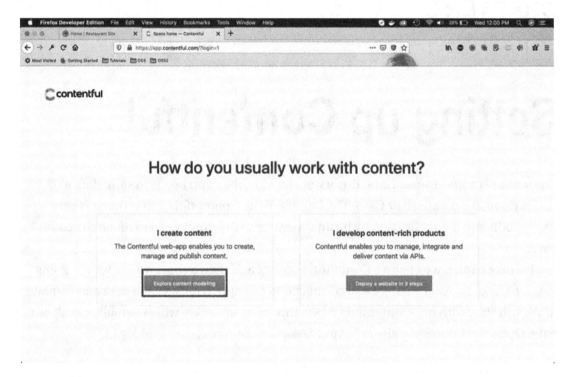

Figure 3-1. *Explore content modeling button*

After that the pop-up window shown in Figure 3-2 will open. It will take some time to prepare. We need to click Explore the example project.

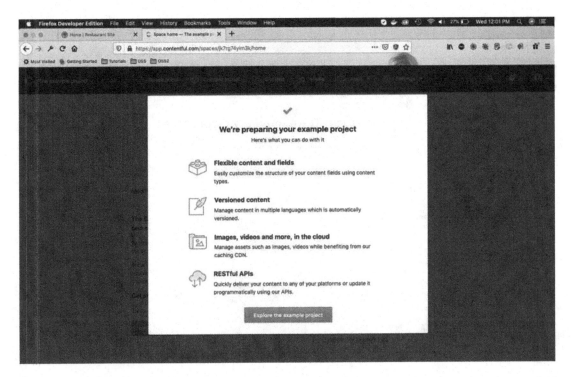

Figure 3-2. *Example project*

That will take us to the screen shown in Figure 3-3. We need to delete this example project, though, because the free tier of Contentful CMS allows us only two projects.

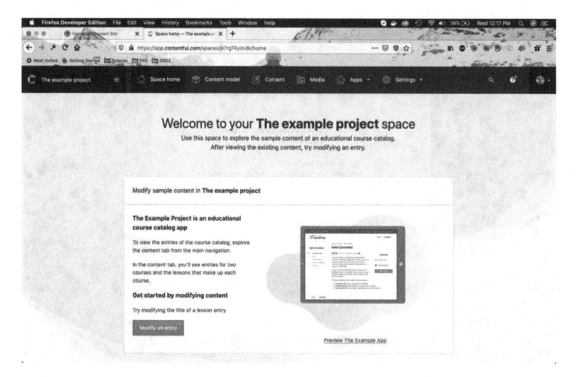

Figure 3-3. *Example app*

On the menu bar, click Settings ➤ General Settings to begin the process of deleting this app (Figure 3-4).

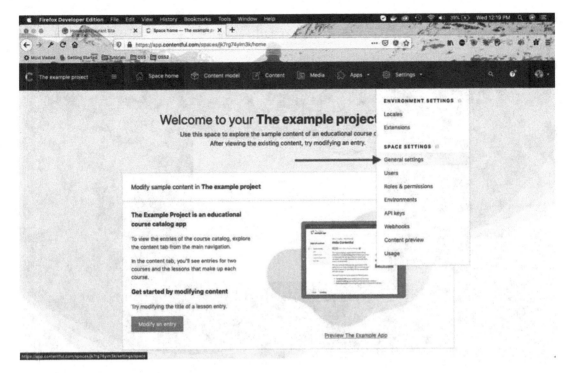

Figure 3-4. *General settings*

On the next screen, you will be shown the Space settings. Click Remove space and all its contents (Figure 3-5).

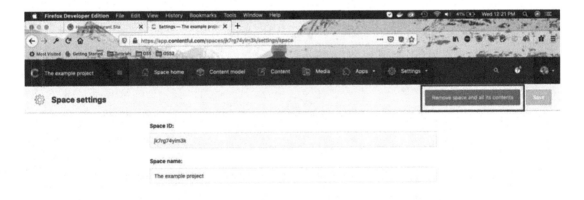

Figure 3-5. *Remove space*

In the pop-up window that appears, type the space name, which in this case is The example project, and then click Remove (Figure 3-6).

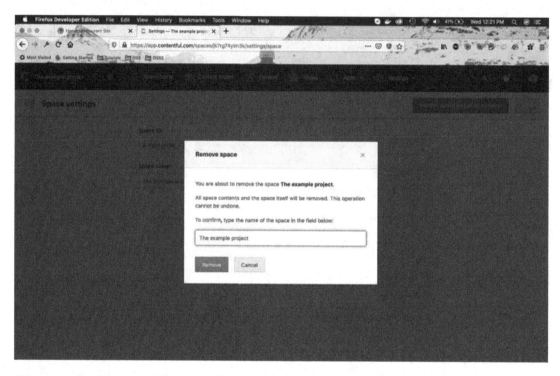

Figure 3-6. *Remove the example project space*

After the example project is removed, the screen shown in Figure 3-7 will open. Click Add a space.

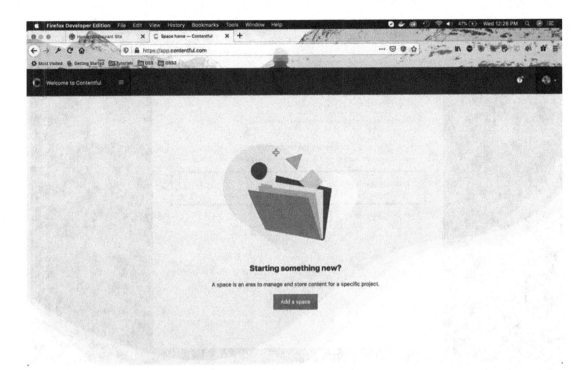

Figure 3-7. *Add a space*

On the next screen, select the Free space type, as shown in Figure 3-8.

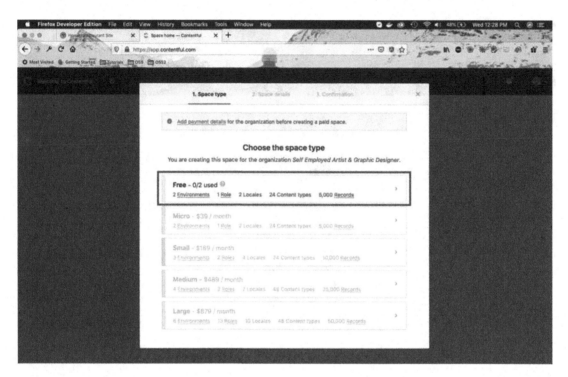

Figure 3-8. *Selecting the Free space type*

Enter a space name (restaurant for our example) in the next pop-up window and click Proceed to confirmation (Figure 3-9).

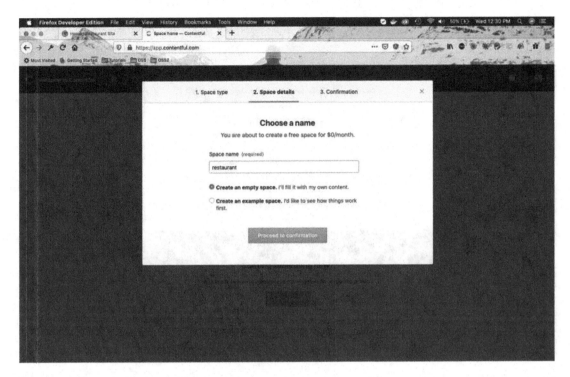

Figure 3-9. *Assigning a Space name*

On the next screen, click Confirm and create a space (Figure 3-10).

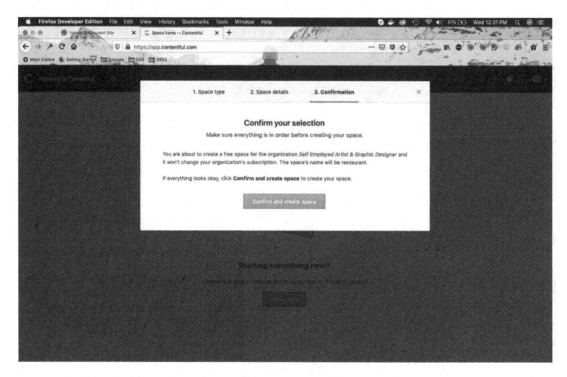

Figure 3-10. *Confirm the selection*

You will be then see the Space home screen (Figure 3-11).

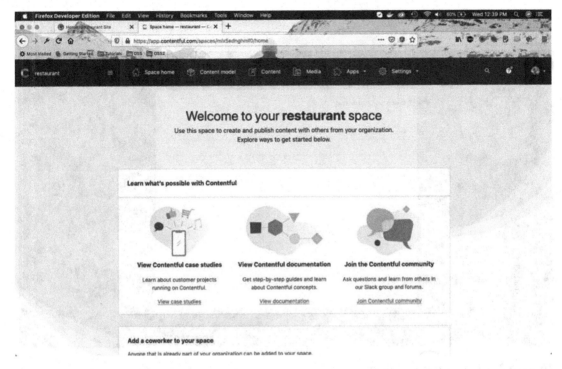

Figure 3-11. *Space home*

Click Content on the menu bar, then click Add Content Type. After that the pop-up window shown in Figure 3-12 opens. Fill in the requested details and click Create.

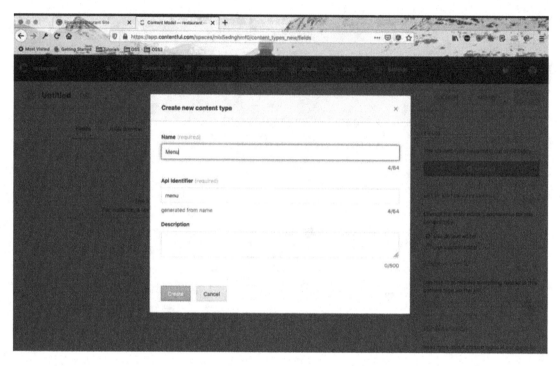

Figure 3-12. *Providing details*

On the next screen, click Add Field to open the pop-up window shown in Figure 3-13. Click the Text field.

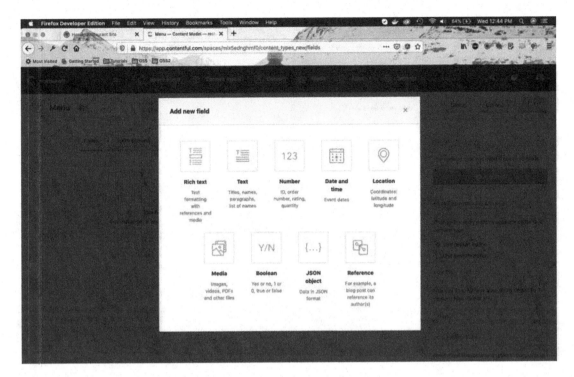

Figure 3-13. *Adding a new field*

After that, enter the details, which will be name in our case, and click Create
(Figure 3-14).

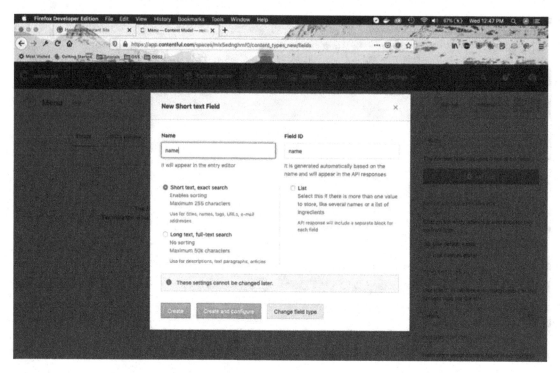

Figure 3-14. Entering field details

Again click Add Field button and then select Number. In the next pop-up window, enter the name as price, select Decimal, and then click Create (Figure 3-15).

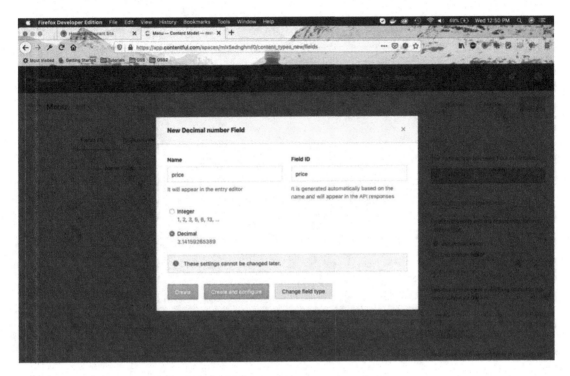

Figure 3-15. *Adding a price field*

Click Add Field again and then select Text. Enter the name as ingredients and click Create (Figure 3-16).

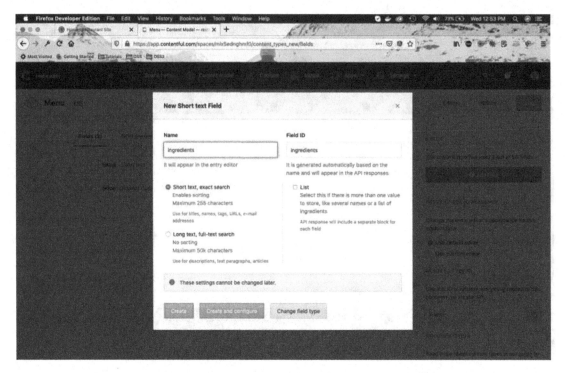

Figure 3-16. *Adding an ingredients field*

Again click Add Field and then select Media. Enter the name img and click Create
(Figure 3-17).

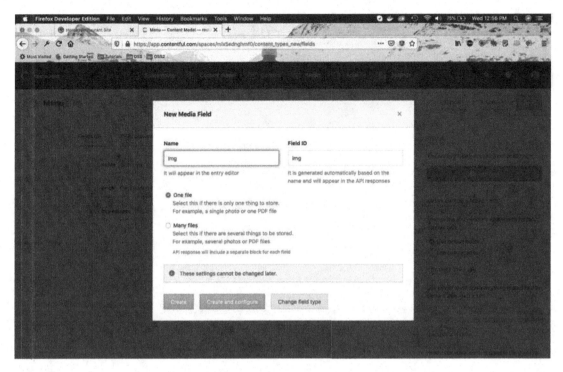

Figure 3-17. *Adding an img image field*

We have finished creating our content model, so click Save (Figure 3-18).

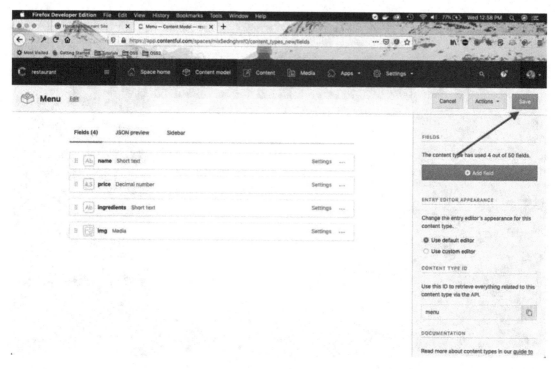

Figure 3-18. *Saving the model*

Adding Items

We will continue setting up Contentful, which we started in the previous section. Click Content tab and click Add Menu (Figure 3-19).

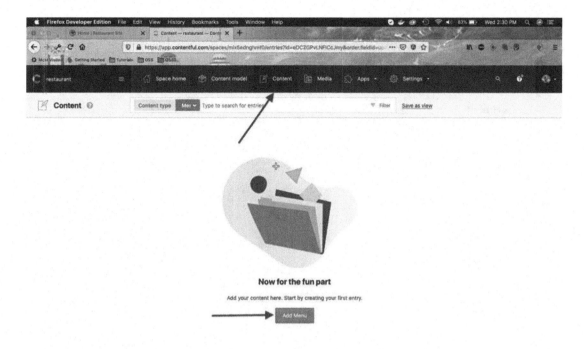

Figure 3-19. *Adding a menu*

On the next screen, enter values for the the name, price, and ingredients fields. After that, click Create new asset and link to add an image (Figure 3-20).

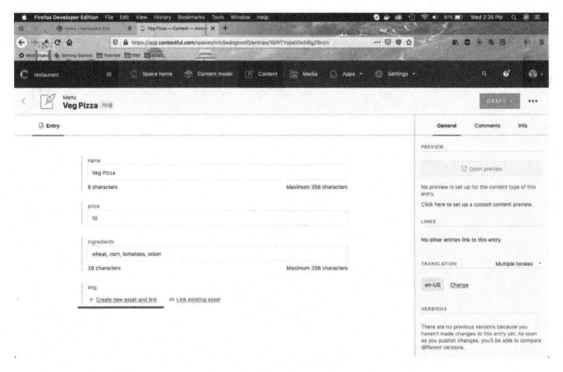

Figure 3-20. *Veg pizza menu item*

On the next screen, in the pop-up window that opens, click Open file selector (Figure 3-21).

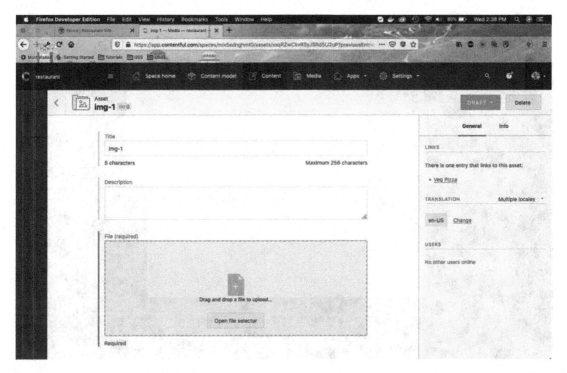

Figure 3-21. *Open file selector*

After that, another pop-up will open. Click Select Files to Upload and select the file you want to use (Figure 3-22).

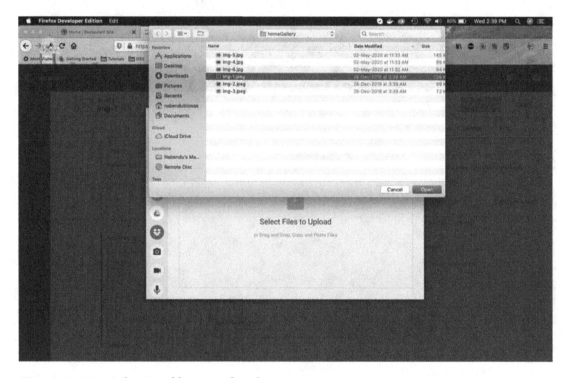

Figure 3-22. *Selecting files to upload*

Next, it will show that our image has been loaded. Click DRAFT and then click
Publish. After that, go back the the previous screen by clicking the left arrow button
(Figure 3-23).

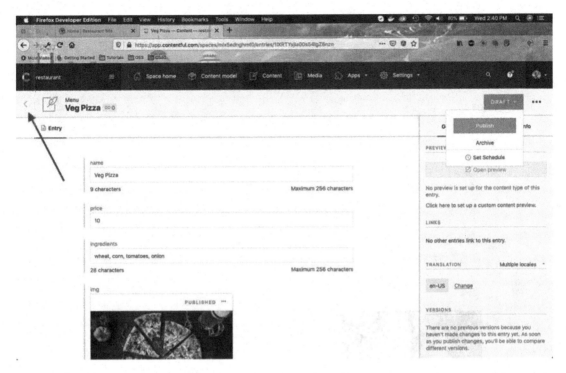

Figure 3-23. *Publishing a draft*

Next, on the main page, again click DRAFT and then click Publish (Figure 3-24).

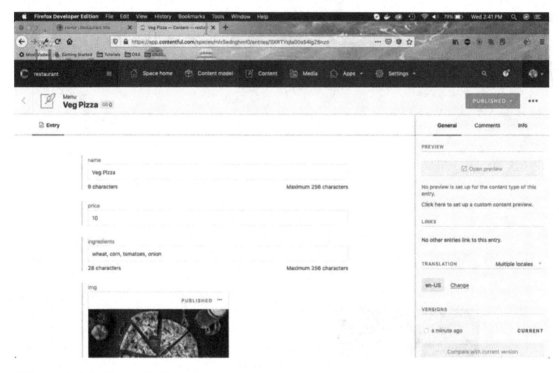

Figure 3-24. *Published item*

You can add more items following the same procedure. Once we are on the main Content screen, click Add Menu to add new items (Figure 3-25).

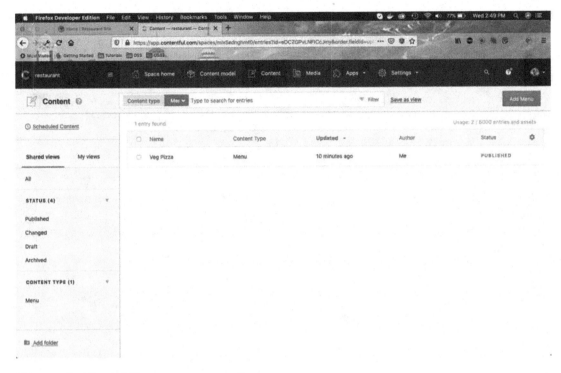

Figure 3-25. *Adding more menu items*

In the example shown in Figure 3-26, I have added ten additional Menu items, as displayed on the Content page.

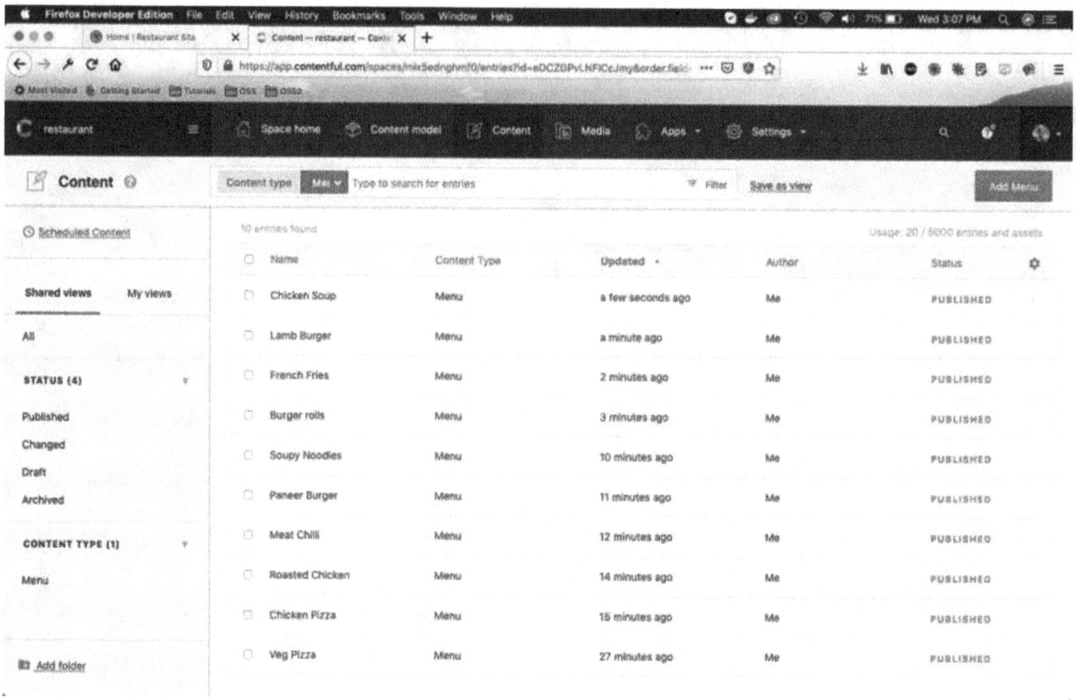

Figure 3-26. *Menu items added*

API Keys

Now that we have added all the items, it is time to configure the API keys that we are going to use in our code. Click Settings and then click API keys (Figure 3-27).

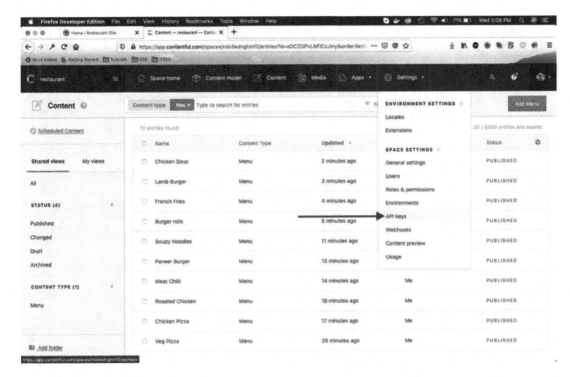

Figure 3-27. *API keys*

On the next screen, select Example Key 1, as we want to change its name (Figure 3-28).

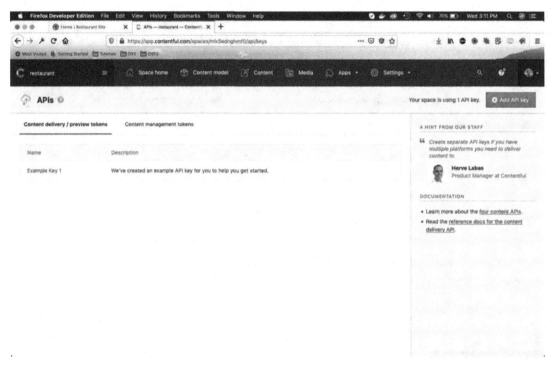

Figure 3-28. *Example Key 1*

You can name this key anything you like, but I named it menu. Once you have entered the name, click Save. You need to note the Space ID and the Content Delivery API — access token for future use in the code (Figure 3-29).

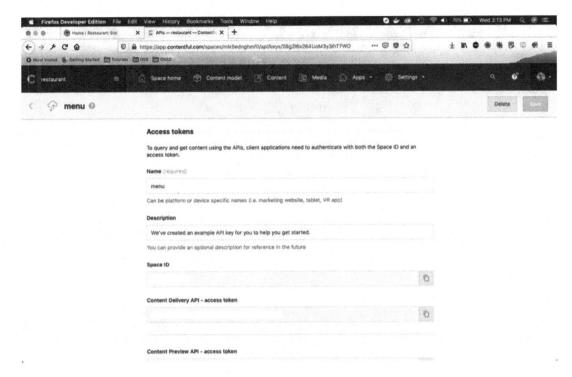

Figure 3-29. *Using menu as the API key name*

API Keys in Code

We have completed adding data to our Contentful CMS in the past two sections.
Now, to use those data we have to first install a Gatsby plug-in called gatsby-source-
contentful, available at `https://www.gatsbyjs.org/packages/gatsby-source-`
`contentful/?=contentfu`. Now, as per the documentation, we have to do an `npm`
`install` first, followed by adding lines in the `gatsby- config.js` file (Figure 3-30).

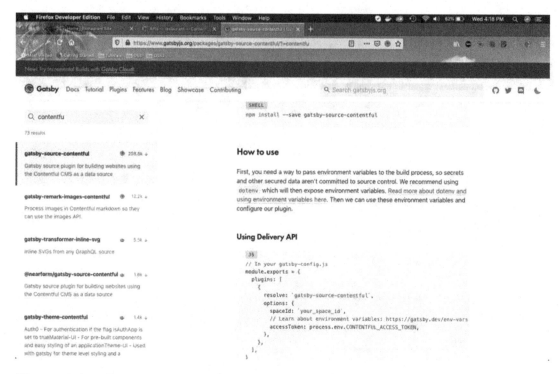

Figure 3-30. *Preparing to use data*

First, stop your `gatsby develop` and install it through `npm install --save`
`gatsby-source-contentful`. As per the documentation, we are also adding the code
in Listing 3-1 to the `gatsby-config.js` file.

Listing 3-1. `gatsby-config.js`

```
module.exports = {
  siteMetadata: {
  ...
  ...
  },
  plugins: [
  ...
  ...
  {
    resolve: `gatsby-plugin-styled-components`,
    options: {
```

```
      // Add any options here
    },
  },
  {
    resolve: `gatsby-source-contentful`,
    options: {
      spaceId: `your_space_id`,
      accessToken: process.env.CONTENTFUL_ACCESS_TOKEN,
    },
  },
  {
    resolve: `gatsby-plugin-manifest`,
    options: {
      name: `gatsby-starter-default`,
      short_name: `starter`,
      start_url: `/`,
      background_color: `#663399`,
      theme_color: `#663399`,
      display: `minimal-ui`,
      icon: `src/images/gatsby-icon.png`, // This path is relative to the
                                          root of the site.
    },
  },
  ],
}
```

Now, we need to include our Space ID and access token from Contentful here. We shouldn't put that information here directly and make it public via GitHub, however. We will store it in an environment file and access it from there. To do that, first put the lines in Listing 3-2 shown in bold at the top of the gatsby-config.js file.

Listing 3-2. gatsby-config.js

```
require('dotenv').config({
  path: `.env.${process.env.NODE_ENV}`,
})
```

```
module.exports = {
  siteMetadata: {
    title: `Restaurant Site`,
    description: `The Restaurant Site`,
    author: `@thewebdev`,
  },
...
...
}
```

After that, create an `.env.development` file in the root directory and also add a `.gitignore` file, so that it is not pushed to GitHub. The updated content is shown in bold in Listing 3-3.

Listing 3-3. `.gitignore`

```
# Logs
logs
*.log
npm-debug.log*
yarn-debug.log*
yarn-error.log*
.env.development
# Runtime data
pids
*.pid
*.seed
*.pid.lock
...
...
```

Now, open the `.env.development` file and put two variables in it, ACCESS_TOKEN and SPACE_ID. You can find the value of both of these on the Contentful site. We created them in the last section.

```
ACCESS_TOKEN=<your access token>
SPACE_ID=<your space id>
```

Now, let's update them in the `gatsby-config.js` file. The updated content is shown in bold in Listing 3-4.

Listing 3-4. gatsby-config.js

```
require('dotenv').config({
  path: `.env.${process.env.NODE_ENV}`,
})

module.exports = {
…

…

    {
      resolve: `gatsby-plugin-styled-components`,
      options: {
        // Add any options here
      },
    },
    {
      resolve: `gatsby-source-contentful`,
      options: {
        spaceId: process.env.SPACE_ID,
        accessToken: process.env.ACCESS_TOKEN,
      },
    },
    {
    …

    …

    },
    },
  ],
}
```

Now, restart your `gatsby develop` and if everything is okay, you will get no errors. We will also get the message that it is connected to Contentful and data have been retrieved. We also need to put these API keys in our Netlify. Open your Netlify account and go to the site. After that, click Deploys and then click Deploy settings (Figure 3-31).

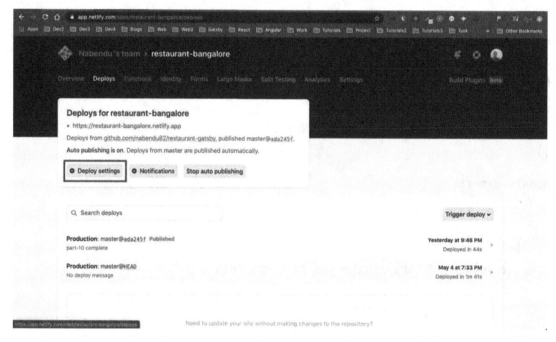

Figure 3-31. *Adding the API keys to Netlify*

Scroll down a bit and you will find the Environment variables section. Click Edit variables (Figure 3-32).

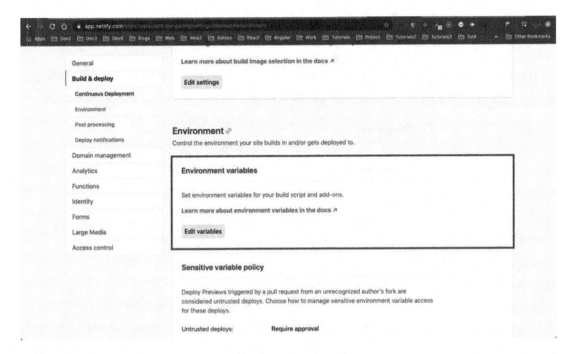

Figure 3-32. *Environment variables*

Now, we can add both our ACCESS_TOKEN and SPACE_ID, along with their values, and click Save (Figure 3-33).

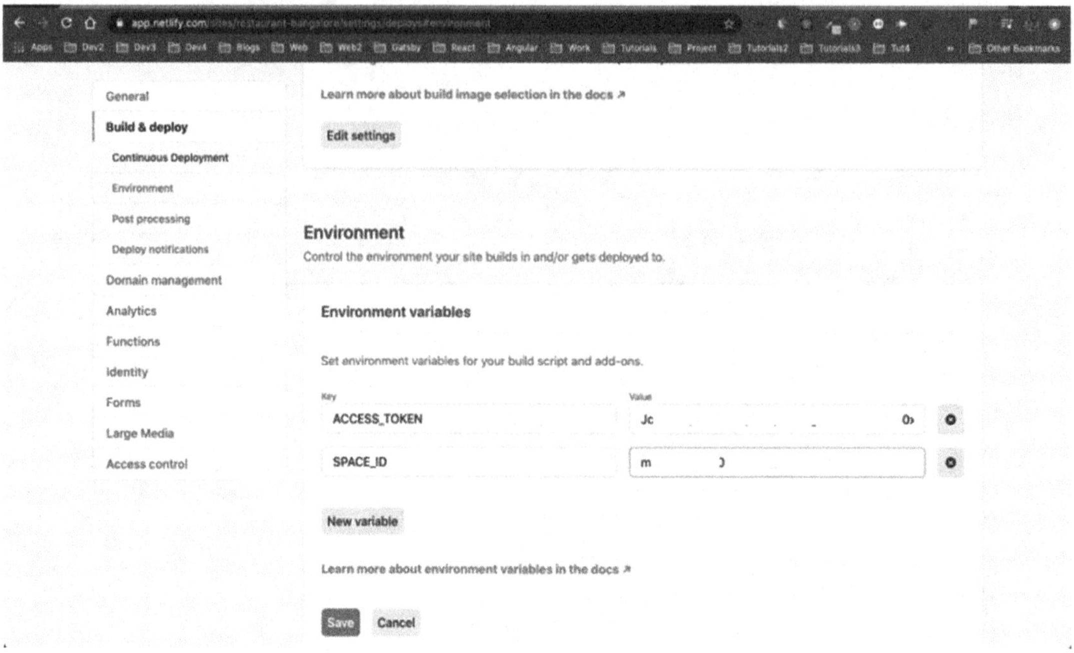

Figure 3-33. *Access tokens*

Showing Items

We will start to show the data from Contentful in our site in this part. Create a file named Menu.js inside the HomeComponents folder and put the content given in Listing 3-5 in the file. Here, we are again using useStaticQuery to get all the data from graphql. After we retrieve the data, we store it in const edges.

Listing 3-5. Menu.js

```
import React from 'react'
import { useStaticQuery, graphql } from 'gatsby'
import { Section, Title, SectionButton } from '../../utils'
import styled from 'styled-components'
import { Link } from 'gatsby'

const Menu = () => {
    const data = useStaticQuery(graphql`
        {
```

```
        items: allContentfulMenu {
            edges {
                node {
                    name
                    price
                    id
                    ingredients
                    img {
                        fixed(width: 150, height: 150) {
                            ...GatsbyContentfulFixed_tracedSVG
                        }
                    }
                }
            }
        }
    `)
    const { edges } = data.items;
    console.log(edges);
    return <div>Menu</div>
}

export default Menu;
```

We also need to add this Menu component to index.js in the pages folder. The updated code for this is shown in bold in Listing 3-6.

Listing 3-6. index.js

```
...
...
import Gallery from '../components/HomeComponents/Gallery'
import Menu from '../components/HomeComponents/Menu'

const IndexPage = () => (
  <Layout>
    <SEO title="Home" />
    <HomeHeader img={img}>
```

123

```
      <Banner title="Fine Dining" subtitle="65, MG Road- Bangalore, KA">
        <BannerButton style={{ margin: '2rem auto' }}>menu</BannerButton>
      </Banner>
    </HomeHeader>
    <QuickInfo />
    <Gallery />
    <Menu />
  </Layout>
)

export default IndexPage
```

Now, when we check in localhost, we can find in the console that we are getting our ten items from Contentful (Figure 3-34).

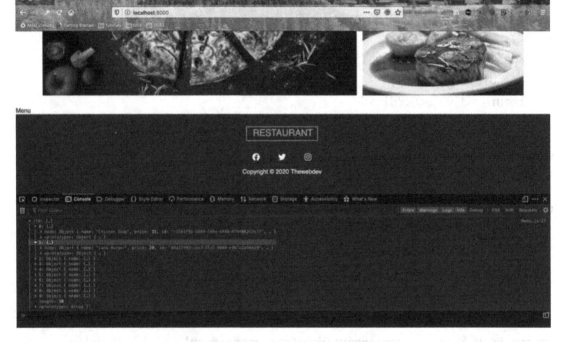

Figure 3-34. *localhost*

Now, let's move back to Menu.js and add code to loop through edges, and pass the data about individual items to a new Product component. The updated code for this is shown in bold in Listing 3-7.

Listing 3-7. Importing a product component to `Menu.js`

```
import Product from './Product'

...

...
    const { edges } = data.items;
    console.log(edges);
    return (
      <Section>
        <Title title="featured items" message="little taste" />
        <ProductList>
            {edges.map(item => {
                return <Product key={item.node.id} product={item.node} />
            })}
        </ProductList>
      </Section>
    )
}

export const ProductList = styled.div``;

export default Menu;
```

Let's quickly create a `Product.js` file in the same directory and put the initial code given in Listing 3-8 in the file.

Listing 3-8. `Product.js`

```
import React from 'react'

const Product = () => {
  return (
    <div>
      Product
    </div>
  )
}

export default Product
```

Now, our home page will display ten times the text product, from the Product component (Figure 3-35).

Figure 3-35. *Product display*

Let's complete the styles for this ProductList component in the Menu.js file. The updated code for this is shown in bold in Listing 3-9.

Listing 3-9. Completing the styles in Menu.js

```
export const ProductList = styled.div`
    margin: 3rem 0;
    display: grid;
    grid-template-columns: 100%;
    grid-row-gap: 3rem;
    @media (min-width: 576px) {
        display: grid;
        grid-template-columns: 95%;
    }
```

```
@media (min-width: 776px) {
    grid-template-columns: 80%;
    justify-content: center;
}
@media (min-width: 992px) {
    grid-template-columns: 1fr 1fr;
    grid-gap: 2rem;
}
```

```
export default Menu;
```

Now, let's complete the Product.js file, so that we can see some nice products on the home page. Here, we are just taking the individual product and displaying it. Now, let's style the ProductWrapper styled-component. The complete code for this is given in Listing 3-10.

Listing 3-10. Complete code for Product.js

```
import React from 'react'
import styled from 'styled-components'
import { styles } from '../../utils'
import Img from 'gatsby-image'
const Product = ({ product }) => {
    const { name, price, ingredients } = product
    const { fixed } = product.img

    return (
        <ProductWrapper>
            <Img fixed={fixed} className="img" />
            <div className="text">
                <div className="product-content">
                    <h3 className="name">{name}</h3>
                    <h3 className="price">${price}</h3>
                </div>
                <p className="info">{ingredients}</p>
            </div>
```

```
        </ProductWrapper>
    )
}

export const ProductWrapper = styled.div`
    @media (min-width: 576px) {
        display: grid;
        grid-template-columns: auto 1fr;
        grid-column-gap: 1rem;
    }
    .img {
        border-radius: 0.5rem;
    }
    .product-content {
        display: flex;
        justify-content: space-between;
        font-size: 1.4rem;
        text-transform: uppercase;
    }
    .name {
        color: ${styles.colors.mainGrey};
        margin-top: 0.5rem;
    }
    .price {
        color: ${styles.colors.mainYellow};
        margin-top: 0.5rem;
    }
    .info {
        margin-top: 0.5rem;
        word-spacing: 0.2rem;
        text-transform: lowercase;
    }
`;

export default Product;
```

Our menu will look like Figure 3-36 on a desktop screen.

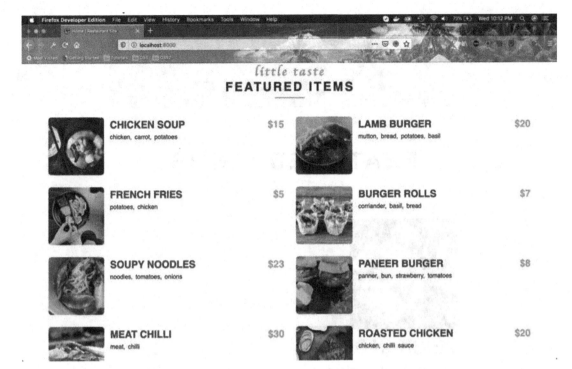

Figure 3-36. *View from a desktop screen*

The menu will appear like Figure 3-37 on a mobile screen.

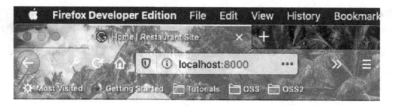

little taste

FEATURED ITEMS

CHICKEN SOUP $15

chicken, carrot, potatoes

LAMB BURGER $20

mutton, bread, potatoes, basil

Figure 3-37.   *View from a mobile screen*

I have pushed the code to GitHub, so it has redeployed the site at Netlify (see `https://restaurant-bangalore.netlify.app/`).

Summary

In this chapter, we created a Contentful account and then a space, where we stored our data. After that we connected it to our app and got the data displayed in our web app. In the next chapter, we will link our Netlify to Contentful CMS using webhooks. This is very helpful if we are creating a site for a client to whom we had only given Contentful access. Now, they can just change the data in Contentful and the site will be redeployed with the required changes.

CHAPTER 4

Using Webhooks at the Site

Webhooks are automated messages sent from apps when something happens; this feature is pending in our site. We have added all menu items, but if we want to change one item or add some new items, after adding the data in Contentful, we have to trigger the deployment in Netlify.

We can automate this process. It helps if we are creating a site with an ecommerce feature for a client to whom we had only given Contentful access. Now, they can just change the data in Contentful and the site will be redeployed with the change.

We are going to link webhooks in our Netlify dashboard for this application. Right now, whenever we push some code to GitHub, it automatically triggers a build in Netlify and our site gets updated. With this system, however, when a user adds, deletes, or edits some items in Contentful CMS, it will trigger a build of the site.

Getting Started

Let's head over to Netlify for our site and click on Site settings (shown in Figure 4-1).

© Nabendu Biswas 2021
N. Biswas, *Advanced Gatsby Projects*, https://doi.org/10.1007/978-1-4842-6640-3_4

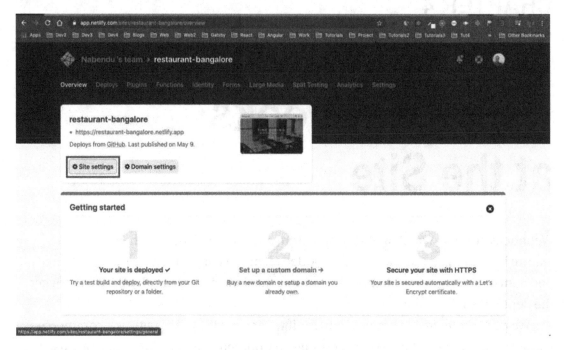

Figure 4-1. *Site settings*

Next, click on the Build & deploy tab and then scroll down to the Build hooks section. There, click Add build hook (Figure 4-2).

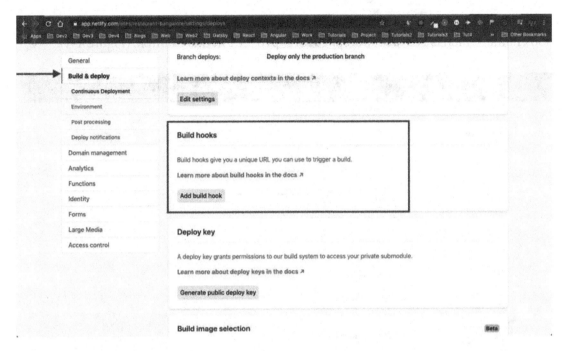

Figure 4-2. *Add build hook*

After that enter a unique name for the hook and click Save (Figure 4-3).

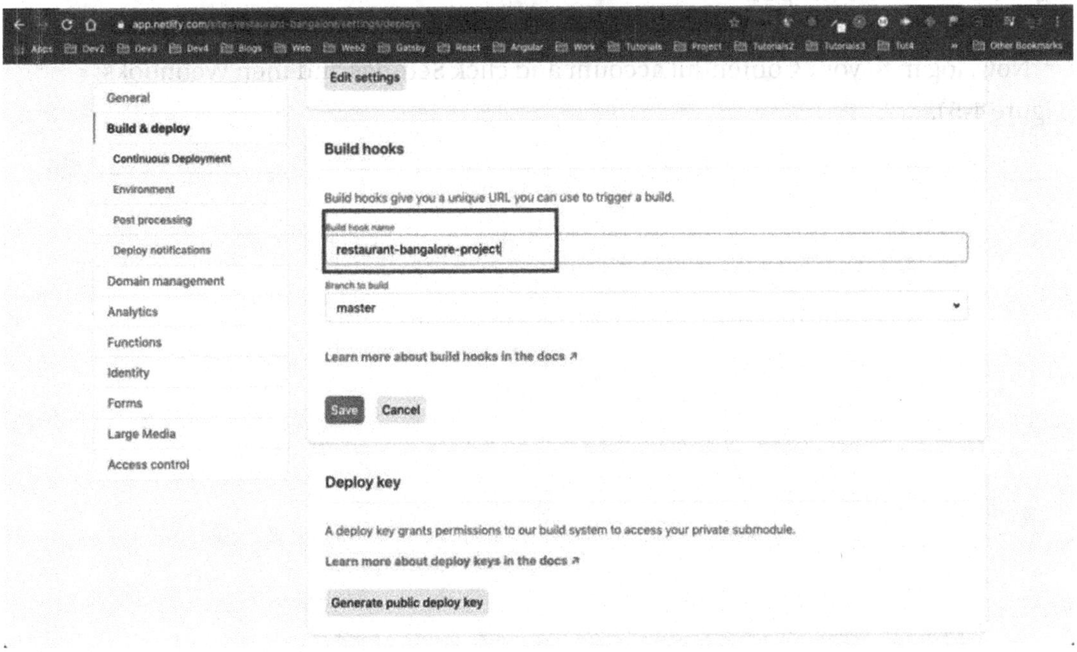

Figure 4-3. *Assign a hook name*

Then, Netlify will assign a unique API endpoint. Note it down along with the Build hook name, which is `restaurant-bangalore-project` in this example (Figure 4-4).

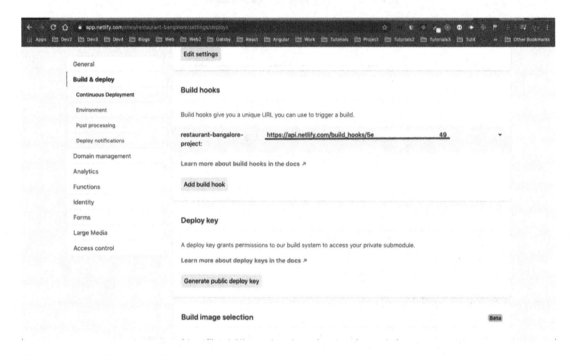

Figure 4-4. *Hook endpoint*

Now, log in to your Contentful account and click Settings and then Webhooks (Figure 4-5).

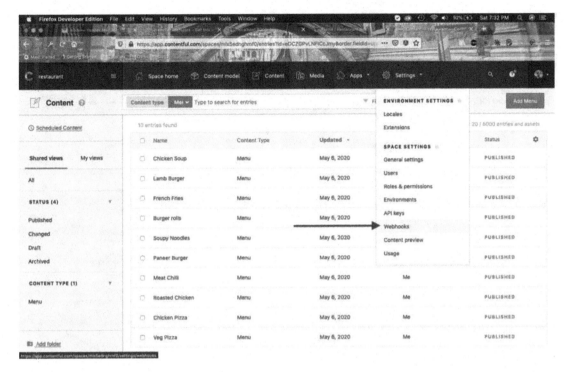

Figure 4-5. *Contentful webhooks*

On right side of the the next screen, click Add Webhook (Figure 4-6).

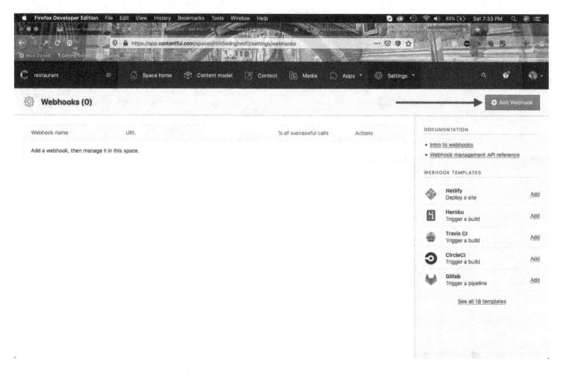

Figure 4-6. *Adding a webhook*

Now, in the Name field, enter the Build hook name from Netlify and provide the URL from Netlify in the URL field (Figure 4-7).

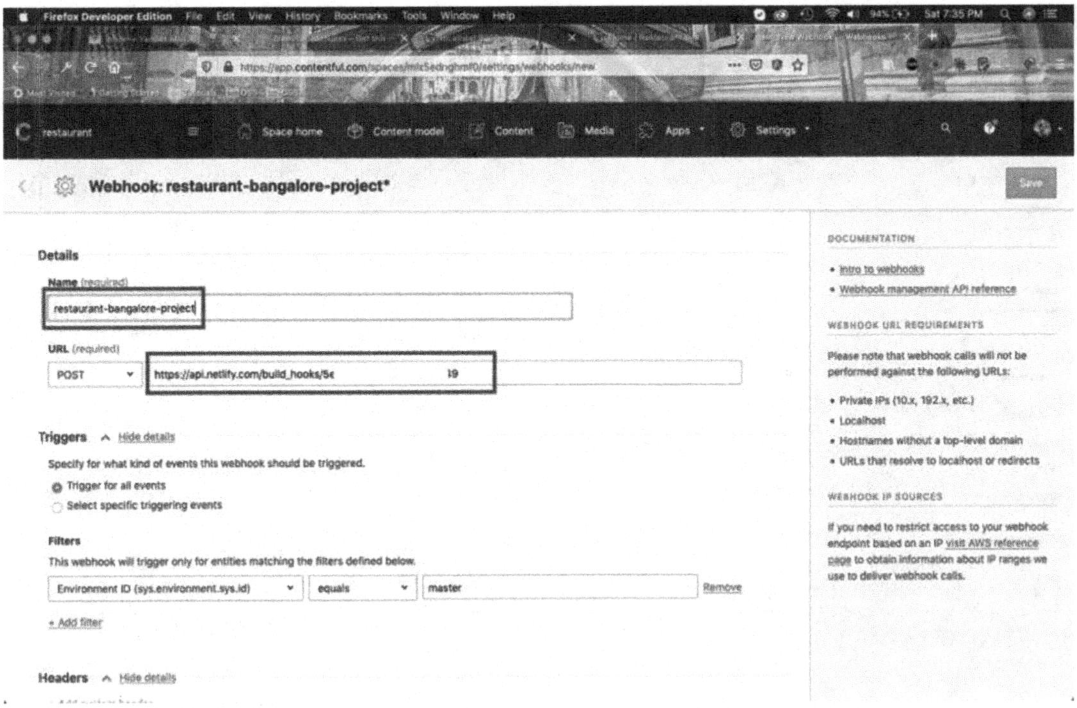

Figure 4-7. *Providing the URL*

Next, click Content and then select French Fries, as we will change some data this entry (Figure 4-8).

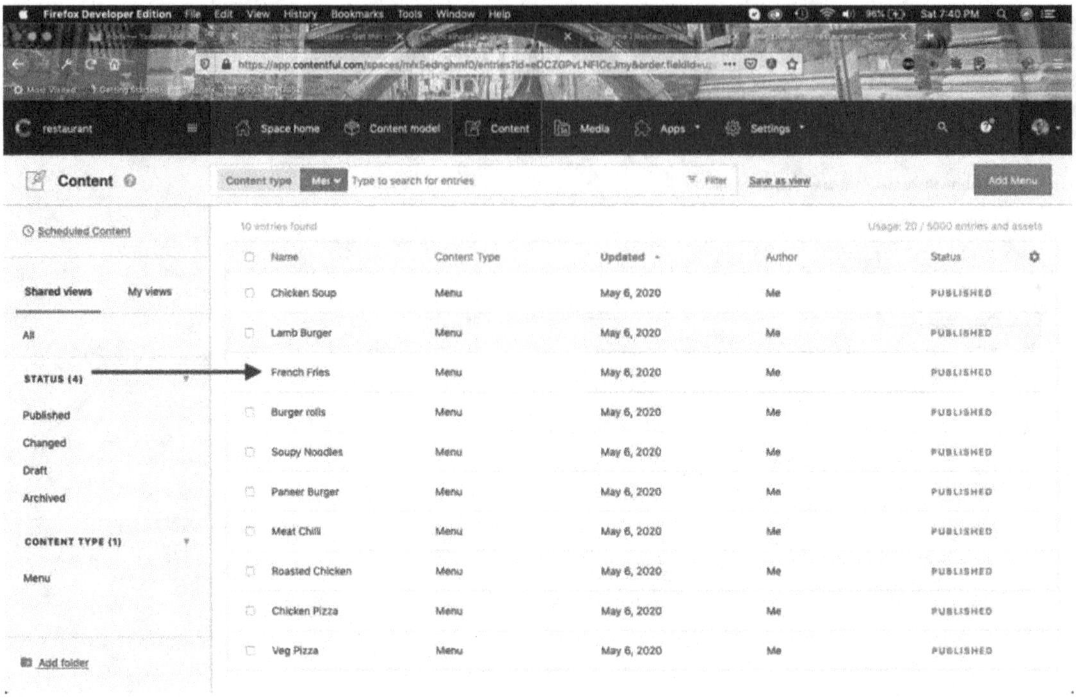

Figure 4-8. *Selecting an entry to edit*

Next, change the ingredients field to include Potatoes, oil, salt from Potatoes, chicken (Figure 4-9).

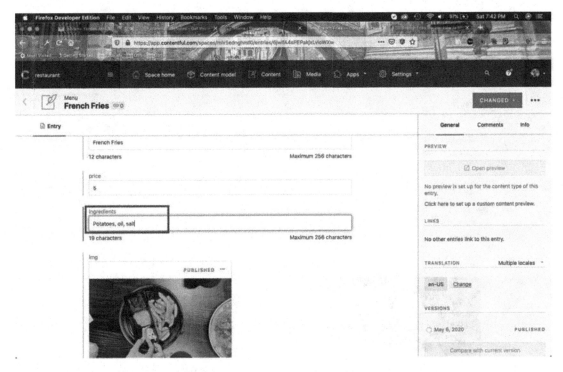

Figure 4-9. *Ingredients changed*

Now, click Changed and select Publish in the drop-down list (Figure 4-10).

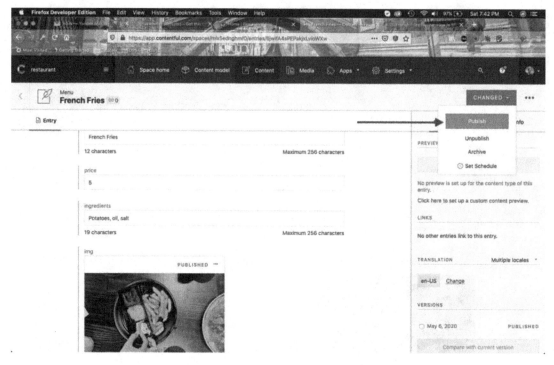

Figure 4-10. *Publish*

Now, when you return to Settings ➤ Webhooks, you will find a new entry there. Click the View details link (Figure 4-11).

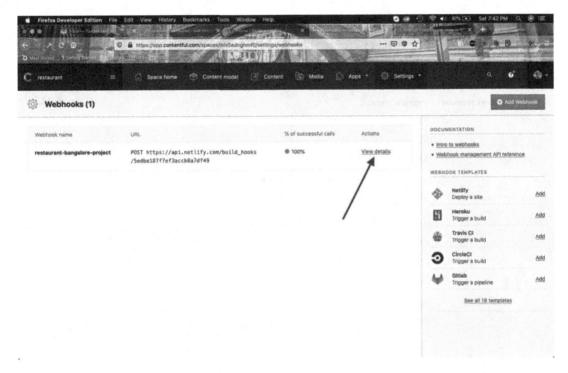

Figure 4-11. *Viewing details*

On the next screen, in the Activity log, click the View details link (Figure 4-12).

Figure 4-12.   *Viewing details*

Now, it will show the response status for the request (Figure 4-13).

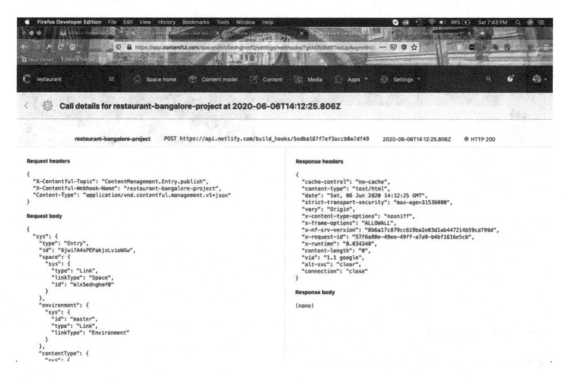

Figure 4-13. *Status*

Now, if return to our Netlify account, we can see the build being triggered by our hook (Figure 4-14).

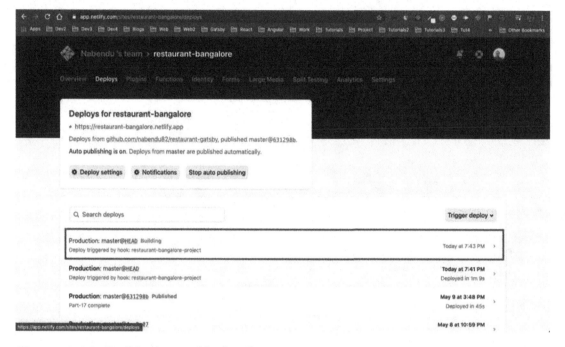

Figure 4-14. *Build triggered by hook*

After the build is done, when we move back to our site, we can see the changes we made reflected on the menu (Figure 4-15).

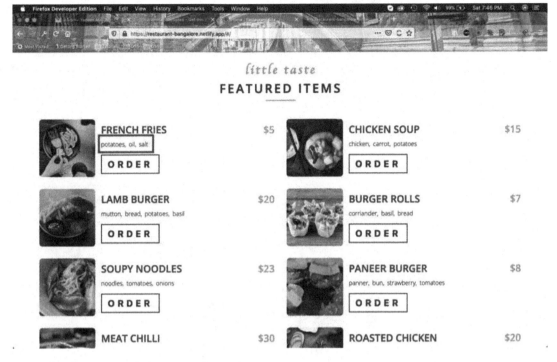

Figure 4-15. *Changes are reflected*

Summary

In this chapter, we added webhooks in our Netlify dashboard for this application. With this, when the user adds, deletes, or edits items in Contentful CMS, it will trigger a build of the site. In the next chapter, we will learn to configure Snipcarst and integrate it in our web app.

CHAPTER 5

Making the Site Dynamic with Snipcart

In the previous chapter, we added webhooks in our Netlify dashboard for this application. With that, when the user adds, deletes, or edits items in the Contentful CMS, it will trigger a build of the site.

In this chapter, we will start to make the static restaurant site an ecommerce site where any user can order food from the menu. We will be using the awesome and easy-to-integrate Snipcart service for this ecommerce feature. In addition to selecting items from the menu, the ecommerce feature will allow users to pay for their orders. The restaurant owner will also get notification of the placed order through email and the Snipcart dashboard.

Adding a Cart Icon

Before we get started with Snipcart, we need to add a cart on the Navbar and buttons beside each menu item.

First, open the `NavbarLinks.js` file inside the `navbar` folder. We need to add `react-icons` for `Cart` and remove the link for `Menu`, because we are showing all menu items on the home page only.

After that let's use the icon after all our links and also make `LinkWrapper` a flex, with everything centered. This is designed for the mobile view.

After that, we will add the styles for the `cart-icon` and also add a `flex-direction: row` for the desktop view. The updated code is shown in bold in Listing 5-1.

© Nabendu Biswas 2021
N. Biswas, *Advanced Gatsby Projects*, https://doi.org/10.1007/978-1-4842-6640-3_5

Listing 5-1. NavbarLinks.js

```
import React, { Component } from 'react'
import styled from 'styled-components'
import { Link } from 'gatsby'
import { styles } from '../../../utils'
import { FaCartArrowDown } from "react-icons/fa"

class NavbarLinks extends Component {
    state = {
        links: [
            {
                id: 0,
                path: '/',
                name: 'home',
            },
            {
                id: 1,
                path: '/about/',
                name: 'about',
            },
            {
                id: 2,
                path: '/contact/',
                name: 'contact',
            },
        ],
    }

    render() {
        return (
            <LinkWrapper open={this.props.navbarOpen}>
                {this.state.links.map(item => {
                    return (
                        <li key={item.id}>
                            <Link to={item.path} className="nav-link">
                                {item.name}
```

```
                                </Link>
                            </li>
                        )
                    })}
                    <FaCartArrowDown className="cart-icon" />
                </LinkWrapper>
            )
        }
}

const LinkWrapper = styled.ul`
    display: flex;
    flex-direction: column;
    justify-content: flex-start;
    align-items: center;
    li {
        list-style-type: none;
    }
    .nav-link {
        display: block;
        text-decoration: none;
        padding: 0.5rem 1rem 0.5rem 1rem;
        color: ${styles.colors.mainGrey};
        font-weight: 700;
        text-transform: capitalize;
        cursor: pointer;
        ${styles.transDefault};
        &:hover {
            background: ${styles.colors.mainGrey};
            color: ${styles.colors.mainYellow};
            padding: 0.5rem 1rem 0.5rem 1.3rem;
        }
    }
    .cart-icon {
        cursor: pointer;
        color: ${styles.colors.mainYellow};
```

```
        font-size: 2rem;
    }
    height: ${props => (props.open ? '152px' : '0px')};
    overflow: hidden;
    ${styles.transObject({ time: '1s' })};
    @media (min-width: 768px) {
        height: auto;
        display: flex;
        flex-direction: row;
        margin: 0 auto;
            .nav-link:hover {
                background: ${styles.colors.mainWhite};
                padding: 0.5rem 1rem 0.5rem 1rem;
            }
    }
`;
```

```
export default NavbarLinks
```

Now, our Navbar will appear as displayed in Figure 5-1 on larger screens with our cart.

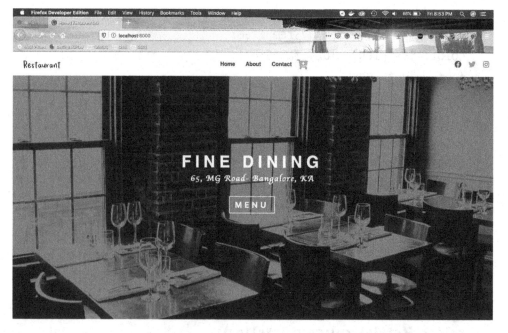

Figure 5-1. *Navbar on a larger screen*

On smaller screens, the Navbar will appear as shown in Figure 5-2.

Figure 5-2. *Navbar on a smaller screen*

Adding an Order Button

Next, let's add a button to order an item for every product. Open the file Product.js and add a SectionButton in it. The updated code is shown in bold in Listing 5-2.

Listing 5-2. Product.js

```
import React from 'react'
import styled from 'styled-components'
import { styles, SectionButton } from '../../utils'
import Img from 'gatsby-image'
const Product = ({ product }) => {
    const { name, price, ingredients } = product
    const { fixed } = product.img

    return (
        <ProductWrapper>
            <Img fixed={fixed} className="img" />
            <div className="text">
                <div className="product-content">
                    <h3 className="name">{name}</h3>
                    <h3 className="price">${price}</h3>
                </div>
                <p className="info">{ingredients}</p>
                <SectionButton>Order</SectionButton>
            </div>
        </ProductWrapper>
    )
}

export const ProductWrapper = styled.div`
...
...
`;

export default Product;
```

Now, the button will display as shown in Figure 5-3 on larger screens.

Figure 5-3. Section button on a larger screen

On mobile screens, it will look like Figure 5-4.

Figure 5-4. *Section button on a mobile screen*

Now, we have all the setup done to get started with Snipcart. We will add it next.

Adding Ecommerce Features

Now that we've prepared the site, let's start to add ecommerce features using Snipcart.

The first step is to sign up for Snipcart at `https://snipcart.com/`. This requires only an email address if you only want to use it for testing. Once you sign up, the dashboard screen (Figure 5-5) will open.

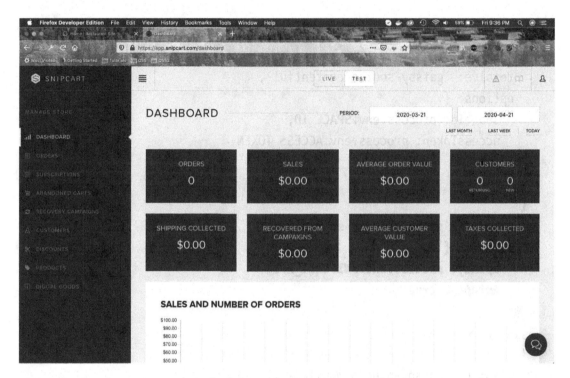

Figure 5-5. *Our ecommerce dashboard*

Before moving forward with the dashboard, we need to install the Gatsby plug-in for Snipcart. We will be using the `gatsby-plugin-snipcartv3` and the documentation for it is available at `https://www.gatsbyjs.org/packages/gatsby-plugin-snipcartv3/?=snipcart`.

Let's stop our `gatsby develop` and `npm install` the plug-in.

```
npm install --save gatsby-plugin-snipcartv3
```

After that, add the plug-in in the `gatsby-config.js` file. The updated code is shown in bold in Listing 5-3.

Listing 5-3. gatsby-config.js

```
require('dotenv').config({
  path: `.env.${process.env.NODE_ENV}`,
})

module.exports = {
...
...
    {
      resolve: `gatsby-source-contentful`,
      options: {
        spaceId: process.env.SPACE_ID,
        accessToken: process.env.ACCESS_TOKEN,
      },
    },
    {
      resolve: 'gatsby-plugin-snipcartv3',
      options: {
        apiKey: process.env.SNIPCART_API,
        autopop: true
      }
    },
    {
      resolve: `gatsby-plugin-manifest`,
      options: {
        name: `gatsby-starter-default`,
        short_name: `starter`,
        start_url: `/`,
        background_color: `#663399`,
        theme_color: `#663399`,
        display: `minimal-ui`,
```

```
    icon: `src/images/gatsby-icon.png`, // This path is relative to the
                                         root of the site.
    },
   },
  ],
}
```

Now, for the API keys, let's go back to the Snipcart dashboard and click the person icon, highlighted in Figure 5-6. After that, scroll a bit down and select API Keys.

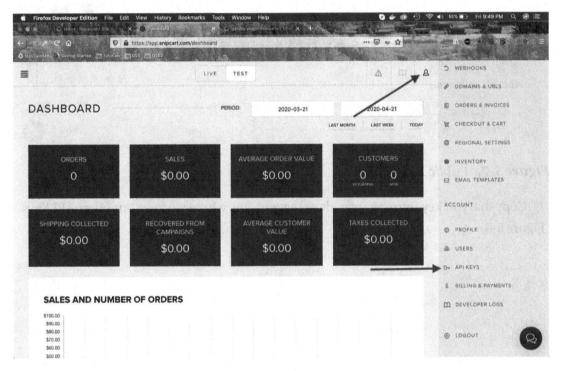

Figure 5-6. *Selecting API Keys*

On the next screen (Figure 5-7), in the Public Test API Key section, you will see the API key, which you need to copy.

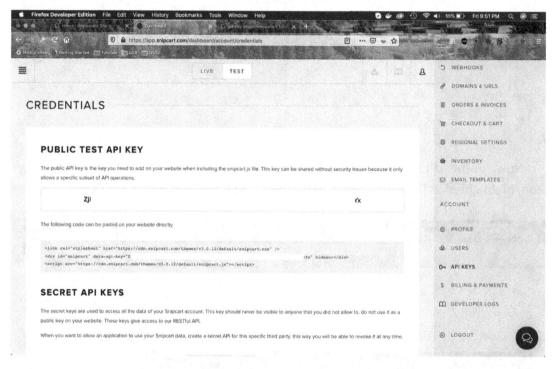

Figure 5-7. *Public test API key*

Copy that API key into the `.env.development` file, where we have our other API Keys (Figure 5-8).

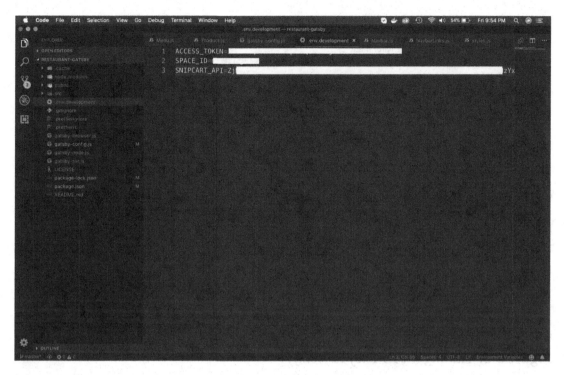

Figure 5-8. *Copying API key to* `.env.development`

We also need to add this API Key in our Netlify account for this site. We will add it using the same process we saw earlier, on the Build & deploy tab under Environment variables (Figure 5-9).

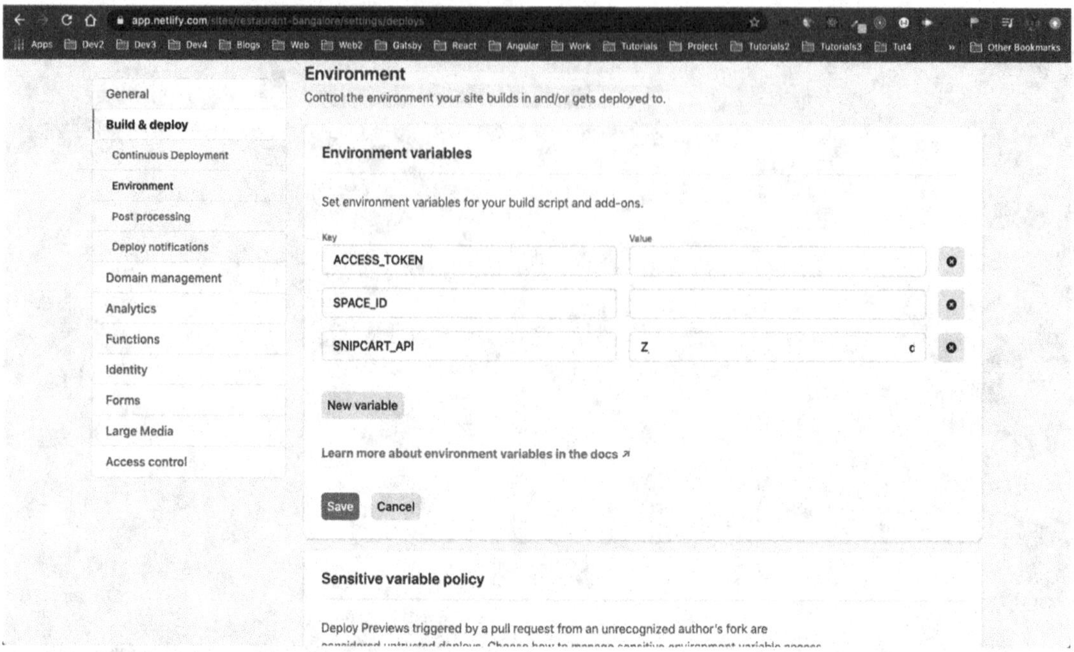

Figure 5-9. *Adding the API key to Netlify*

Now, we need to add cart functionality to our cart in the Navbar. As per the Snipcart documentation (see `https://docs.snipcart.com/v3/setup/cart-summary`), we just need to add `snipcart-checkout` to our `cart` class. Open `NavbarLinks.js` and add the `FaCartArrowDown` class to the file. The updated code is shown in bold in Listing 5-4.

Listing 5-4. `NavbarLinks.js`

```
...
...

class NavbarLinks extends Component {
    state = {
        links: [
        ...
                ],
    }

    render() {
        return (
            <LinkWrapper open={this.props.navbarOpen}>
```

```
            {this.state.links.map(item => {
                return (
                    <li key={item.id}>
                        <Link to={item.path} className="nav-link">
                            {item.name}
                        </Link>
                    </li>
                )
            })}
            <FaCartArrowDown className="cart-icon snipcart-checkout" />
        </LinkWrapper>
    )
  }
}
```

Now, if we go to localhost and click on the cart in Navbar, we will get the overlay shown in Figure 5-10.

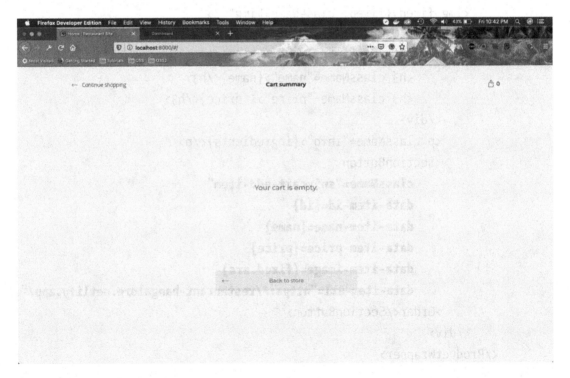

Figure 5-10. *Cart*

Next, we will add the predefined class and data-item to our order button in the Product.js file per the Snipcart documentation at https://docs.snipcart.com/v3/setup/products.

We first need to add the class snipcart-add-item to the button. After that all the other data-items are required. Because we are already getting most of them, we are directly adding them. The URL should be the deployed site URL, because Snipcart crawlers check it. We therefore need to give the exact page where items are located. The updated code is shown in bold in Listing 5-5.

Listing 5-5. Product.js

```
...
const Product = ({ product }) => {
    const { id, name, price, ingredients } = product
    const { fixed } = product.img

    return (
        <ProductWrapper>
            <Img fixed={fixed} className="img" />
            <div className="text">
                <div className="product-content">
                    <h3 className="name">{name}</h3>
                    <h3 className="price">${price}</h3>
                </div>
                <p className="info">{ingredients}</p>
                <SectionButton
                    className="snipcart-add-item"
                    data-item-id={id}
                    data-item-name={name}
                    data-item-price={price}
                    data-item-image={fixed.src}
                    data-item-url="https://restaurant-bangalore.netlify.app/"
                >Order</SectionButton>
            </div>
        </ProductWrapper>
    )
}
```

...

...

In Product.js we are using src to get the image, because we cannot use gatsby-image directly here. Navigate to the parent component of Menu.js and add src to it. The updated code is shown in bold in Listing 5-6.

Listing 5-6. Menu.js

...

```
const Menu = () => {
    const data = useStaticQuery(graphql`
        {
            items: allContentfulMenu {
                edges {
                    node {
                        name
                        price
                        id
                        ingredients
                        img {
                            fixed(width: 150, height: 150) {
                                src
                                ...GatsbyContentfulFixed_tracedSVG
                            }
                        }
                    }
                }
            }
        }
    `)
    const { edges } = data.items;
    console.log(edges);
    return (
        ...
    )
}
```

Now, if we click the order button, it will add the item in our cart (Figure 5-11).

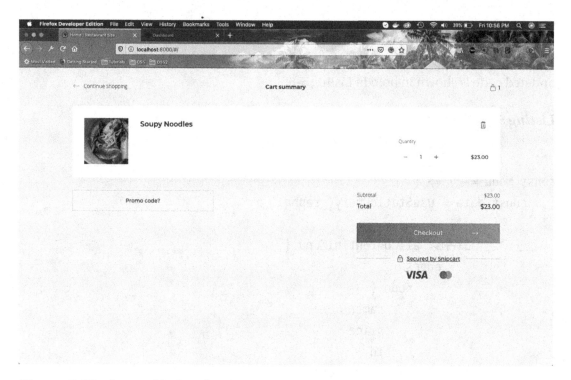

Figure 5-11. Item added to the cart

I am pushing this code to GitHub for automatic deployment to Netlify at `https://restaurant-bangalore.netlify.app`.

After implementing Snipcart earlier in chapter, I had pushed the code to Netlify to deploy the site. While testing payment with a credit card, I got the `errors.error_crawling_failed` error (Figure 5-12).

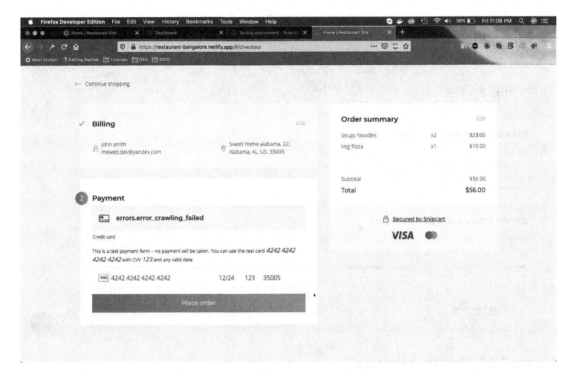

Figure 5-12. *Testing credit card payment and an* `errors.error_crawling_` *failed error*

I contacted Snipcart support for this, and they were prompt to reply, directing me to the documentation at `https://docs.snipcart.com/v3/setup/order-validation`. According to those intructions, I had to add my domain on the Domains & URL page. Once I added it, the whole process was flawless (Figure 5-13).

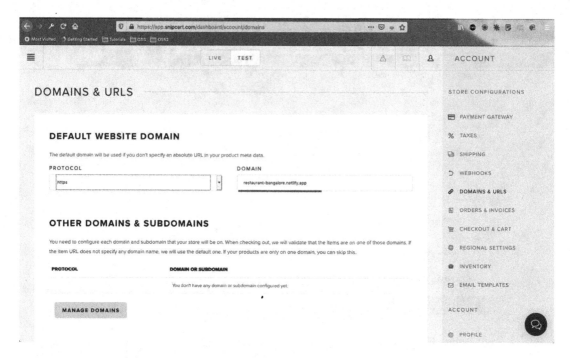

Figure 5-13. *Adding a domain*

Additional Settings

Let's go through the process for my site `https://restaurant-bangalore.netlify.app/#/`.
After adding two items from the site by clicking the Order button, click Checkout on the
screen shown in Figure 5-14.

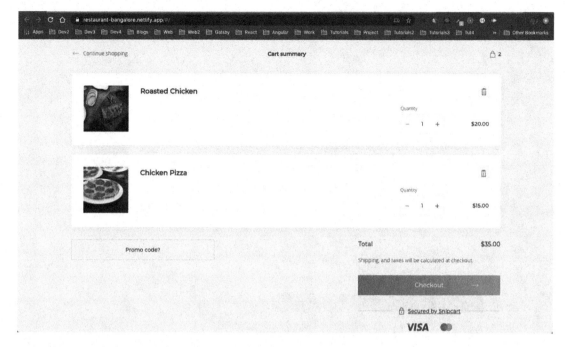

Figure 5-14. *Checking out after an order is placed*

After that, on the next screen enter the name, email, and address, then click Continue to payment (Figure 5-15). Provide a real email address, as that address will receive the order receipt.

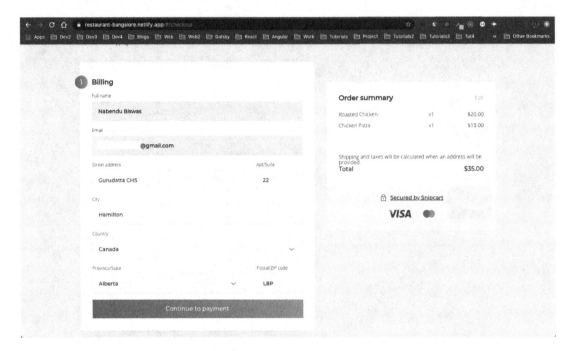

Figure 5-15. *Entering contact information*

On the next screen, enter the test credit card number, which is provided, and click Place order (Figure 5-16).

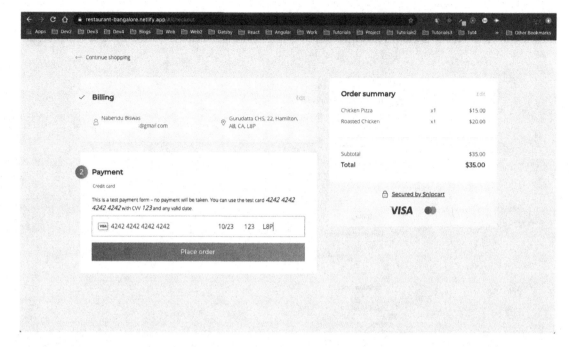

Figure 5-16. *Using a test card*

If payment is successful, the screen shown in Figure 5-17 will display.

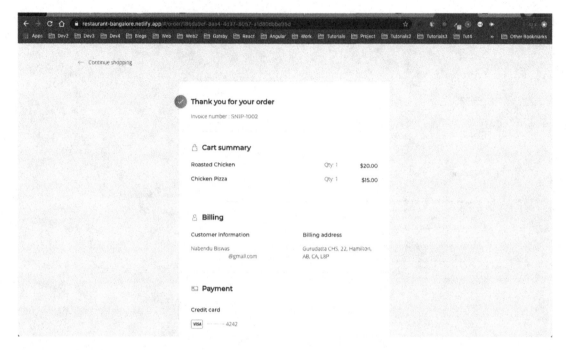

Figure 5-17. *Payment processed successfully*

You should also receive a receipt at the email address entered earlier (Figure 5-18).

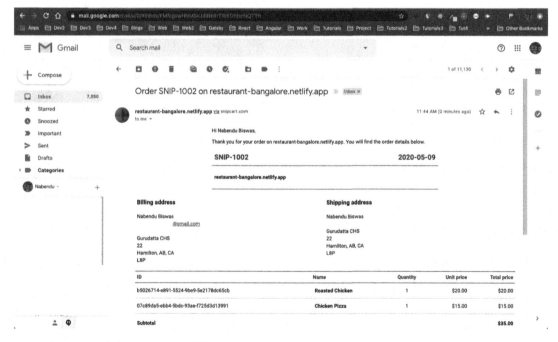

Figure 5-18. *Receipt received*

The orders are also displayed on the Snipcart dashboard (Figure 5-19).

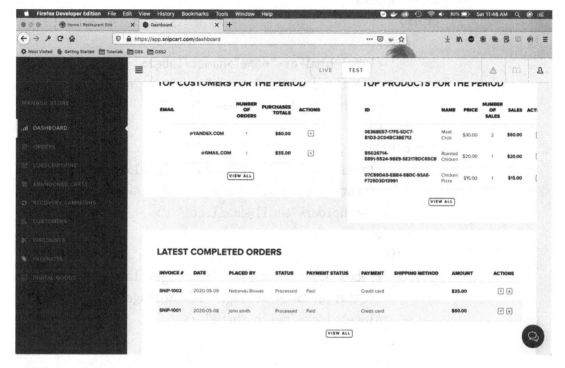

Figure 5-19. *Orders displayed on the dashboard*

Contact Component

Now our site is almost complete, but let's add some content on the About page and also complete the Contact page.

Create a folder named `Contact` inside the `components` folder. Create a file named `Contact.js` inside the `Contact` folder.

Next, add some styles for the form using the code in Listing 5-7.

Listing 5-7. Adding styles to `Contact.js`

```
import React from 'react'
import { styles, Section, SectionButton } from '../../utils'
import styled from 'styled-components'

const Contact = () => {
    return (
```

```
    <Section>
        <ContactWrapper>
            <form>
                <div>
                    <label htmlFor="name">name</label>
                    <input type="text" name="name" id="name"
                    placeholder="john smith" />
                </div>
                <div>
                    <label htmlFor="email">email</label>
                    <input type="email" name="email" id="email"
                    placeholder="email@email.com" />
                </div>
                <div>
                    <label htmlFor="message">message</label>
                    <textarea name="message" id="message" rows="10"
                    placeholder="hello there" />
                </div>
                <div>
                    <SectionButton>Submit</SectionButton>
                </div>
            </form>
        </ContactWrapper>
    </Section>
    )
}

export const ContactWrapper = styled.div`
    width: 80vw;
    margin: 0 auto;
    label {
        text-transform: capitalize;
        font-size: 1.2rem;
        display: block;
        margin-bottom: 0.5rem;
    }
```

```
    input, textarea {
        width: 100%;
        font-size: 1rem;
        margin-bottom: 1rem;
        padding: 0.375rem 0.75rem;
        border: 1px solid ${styles.colors.mainGrey};
        border-radius: 0.25rem;
    }
    @media (min-width: 992px) {
        width: 50vw;
        margin: 0 auto;
    }
`;
export default Contact;
```

Now, we need to use this Contact component in our `contact.js` file in the pages folder. The updated code is shown in bold in Listing 5-8.

Listing 5-8. `contact.js` updated

```
...
import contactImg from '../images/bcg/contactBcg.jpg'
import Contact from '../components/Contact/Contact'

const ContactPage = () => {
  return (
    <Layout>
      <SEO title="Contact" />
      <PageHeader img={contactImg}>
        <Banner title="contact us" subtitle="let's get in touch" />
      </PageHeader>
      <Contact />
    </Layout>
  )
}

export default ContactPage
```

Now, it will display perfectly on our Contact page (Figure 5-20). The form is not completely set up. We can perform the setup easily with the amazing service Formspree (see `https://formspree.io/`), which I have covered in my blog (see `https://medium.com/@nabendu82/the-dev-to-project-with-gatsbyjs-21-c7d176a21710`).

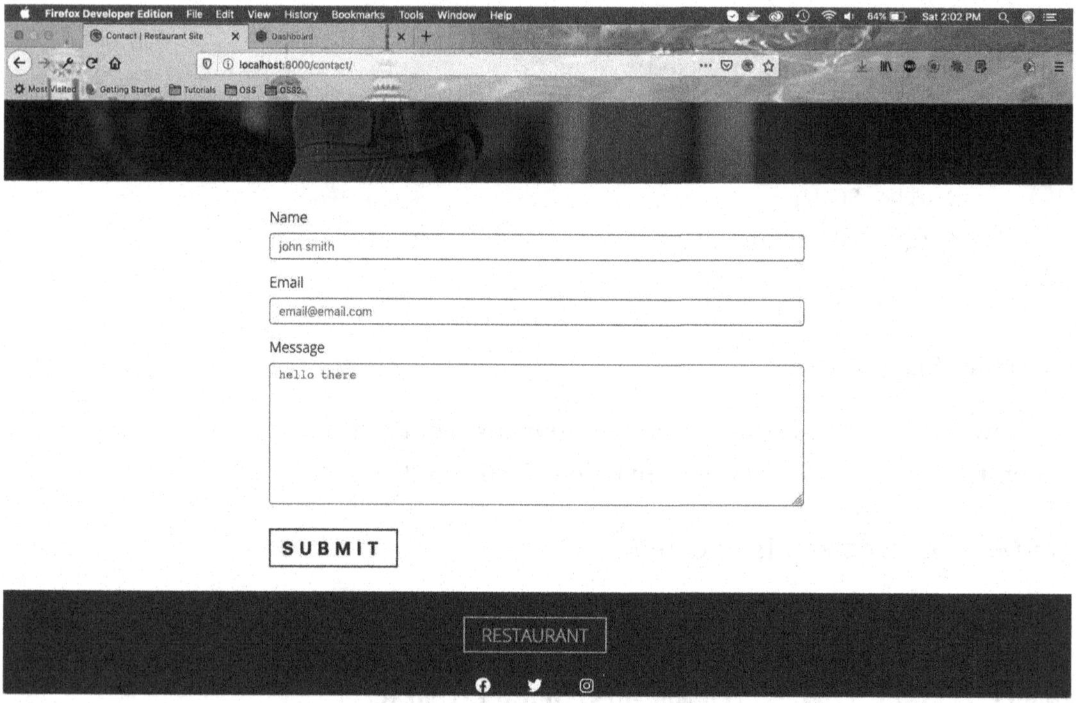

Figure 5-20. *Contact page*

About Component

Let's also complete the About page now. Create a folder named About inside the components folder and add a file named About.js. Now, let's add some styles to the AboutWrapper styled-component. Include the content in Listing 5-9 in the file.

Listing 5-9. Adding styles to About.js

```
import React from 'react'
import { styles, Section } from '../../utils'
import styled from 'styled-components'
```

```
const About = () => {
    return (
        <Section>
            <AboutWrapper>
                <p>At Restaurant, we follow a simple mantra - "Strive for
                continuous improvement and make
                    no compromise on quality!"
                </p>
                <p>Initially we were just a small unit with a handful of
                employees. Today, 13 years later,
                    we have established 6 successful outlets in the city
                    with a strong workforce of about
                    500 people.
                </p>
                <p>
                Providing quality food in perfect hygienic conditions
                remains our top most priority.
                </p>
                <p>
                Our aim is to be easy on the pocket, satiate the ever
                demanding palette and ensure that each customer comes
                back for more.
                </p>
            </AboutWrapper>
        </Section>
    )
}
export const AboutWrapper = styled.div`
    width: 80vw;
    margin: 0 auto;
    p {
        font-size: 1.2rem;
        letter-spacing: 2px;
```

```
        color: ${styles.colors.mainBlack};
        margin-bottom: 2rem;
    }
`;
```

```
export default About;
```

Now, we need to use this About component in our about.js file inside the pages folder. The updated content is shown in bold in Listing 5-10.

Listing 5-10. Updated about.js

```
...
import aboutImg from '../images/bcg/aboutBcg.jpg'
import About from '../components/About/About'

const AboutPage = () => {
  return (
    <Layout>
      <SEO title="About" />
      <PageHeader img={aboutImg}>
        <Banner title="about us" subtitle="a little about us" />
      </PageHeader>
      <About />
    </Layout>
  )
}
```

```
export default AboutPage
```

The About Us page will then display as shown in Figure 5-21.

At Restaurant, we follow a simple mantra - "Strive for continuous improvement and make no compromise on quality!"

Initially we were just a small unit with a handful of employees. Today, 13 years later, we have established 6 successful outlets in the city with a strong workforce of about 500 people.

Providing quality food in perfect hygienic conditions remains our top most priority.

Our aim is to be easy on the pocket, satiate the ever demanding palette and ensure that each customer comes back for more.

Figure 5-21. *About Us page complete*

Let's also change the QuickInfo text and modify its style. Open the `QuickInfo.js` file and make the changes shown in bold in Listing 5-11.

Listing 5-11. `QuickInfo.js`

```
...
import { Link } from 'gatsby'

export default class QuickInfo extends Component {
  render() {
    return (
      <Section>
        <Title message="let us tell you" title="our misson" />
        <QuickInfoWrapper>
          <p className="text">
            Our mission is to provide happiness and joy through food to
            every customer who chooses to dine at Restaurant, while not
            exceeding, making the size of a pin hole on their pockets.
          </p>
```

179

```
        <Link to="/about/" style={{ textDecoration: "none" }}>
          <SectionButton style={{ margin: "2rem auto" }}>about
          </SectionButton>
        </Link>
      </QuickInfoWrapper>
    </Section>
  )
 }
}

const QuickInfoWrapper = styled.div`
    width: 90%;
    margin: 2rem auto;
    .text {
        font-size: 1.2rem;
        letter-spacing: 2px;
        line-height: 2em;
        color: ${styles.colors.mainGrey};
        word-spacing: 0.2rem;
    }

    @media (min-width: 768px) {
        width: 70%;
    }
    @media (min-width: 992px) {
        width: 60%;
    }
`
```

Now, our text on the home page will display as shown in Figure 5-22.

Figure 5-22. Completed home page

Now, this project is complete and ready to be deployed. You can find the instructions for deployment in my blog post at `https://medium.com/@nabendu82/the-dev-to-project-with-gatsbyjs-19-286c48d84ded`.

You can also add many useful Gatsby plug-ins, including Google Analytics. You can find the details on this process in my blog post at `https://medium.com/@nabendu82/the-dev-to-project-with-gatsbyjs-22-6b421c9534ce`.

I hope you like this series and are ready to make some ecommerce sites for yourself or for your clients. You can find the code for the project in the GitHub repo at `https://github.com/nabendu82/restaurant-gatsby`.

Summary

In this chapter, we learned to configure Snipcart and integrate it in our web app. Now our restaurant site is complete with an ecommerce function with which users can order from our menu and pay for their orders. Now it's time to move on to Part II and our next project.

PART II

Creating a Recipe Website with Firebase

Welcome to Part II of the book and a brand new project, where we make a recipe-sharing website using GatsbyJS and Firebase, a Google platform for creating mobile and web applications. The idea of this site came about during the COVID-19 lockdown. My wife made some awesome tasty dishes during this period. She got help from popular YouTube channels to prepare those meals.

In the following chapters we'll cover how to prepare the initial setup of the site, display recipes and images from Firebase with the original YouTube link, and deploy the site in Netlify. The site will also include a Comments section for people to post comments on each dish.

CHAPTER 6

Setting up the Recipe Site

In this chapter, we are going to perform the initial setup for our recipe website. The setup will be mainly done on Firebase website and will also involve setting up the database.

Getting Started

Let's go ahead and create a new site by entering **gatsby new recipes-homemade** in the terminal. Next, let's change the directory and perform `gatsby develop` to run our Gatsby site locally. The following commands should be used:

```
cd recipes-homemade
gatsby develop
```

Now, if we go to `http://localhost:8000/` our site will show the Gatsby default starter (Figure 6-1).

© Nabendu Biswas 2021
N. Biswas, *Advanced Gatsby Projects*, https://doi.org/10.1007/978-1-4842-6640-3_6

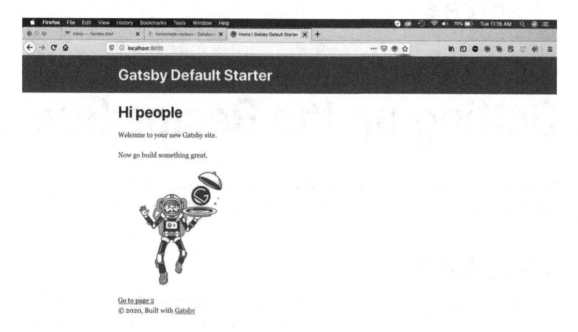

Figure 6-1. *Gatsby default starter*

Setting up Firebase

The next step is to create our Firebase project. Navigate to `https://firebase.google.com/` and sign in with your Google account. After that, click the Go to Console link in the upper right corner of the screen (Figure 6-2).

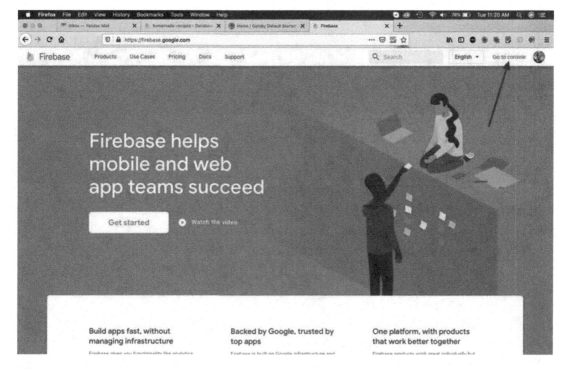

Figure 6-2. *Go to Console*

Click Add Project, which will appear in addition to any other Firebase projects you have (Figure 6-3).

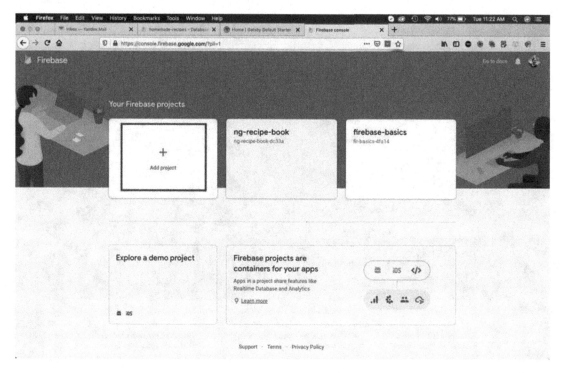

Figure 6-3. *Firebase projects*

On the next screen, enter a name for the project, recipes-homemade in this example. Select the I accept the Firebase terms check box, and then click Continue (Figure 6-4).

Figure 6-4. *Entering a project name*

Next, you need to confirm if want to enable Google Analytics for the project. In this case, we require it, so keep the default settings and click Continue (Figure 6-5).

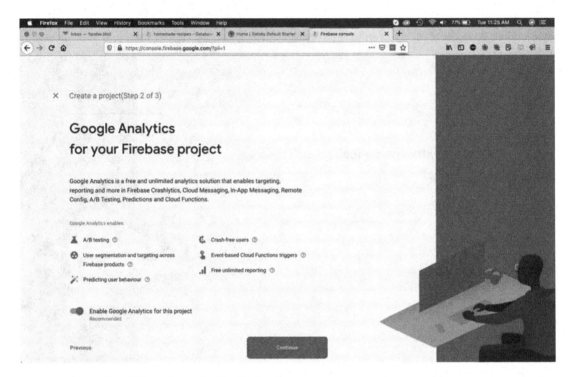

Figure 6-5. *Enabling Google Analytics*

The next step is to select your account. In this example, I am using my wife's Google account. Once your account is selected, click Create Project (Figure 6-6).

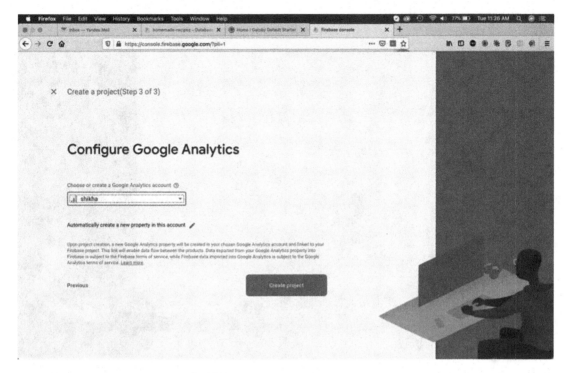

Figure 6-6. *Assigning a Google account*

It will take some time to create the project. During that time, you will see the screen shown in Figure 6-7, which includes a progress bar.

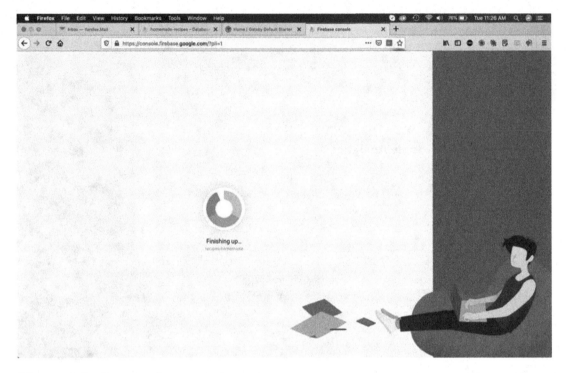

Figure 6-7. *Progress bar*

Once the project is ready, you will be notified on the screen, as shown in Figure 6-8. Click Continue to move to the next step.

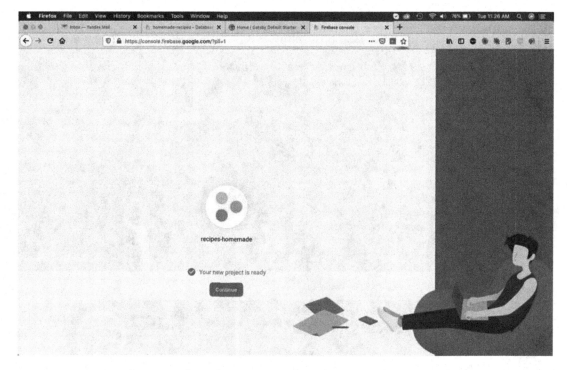

Figure 6-8. Notification that the project is ready

The welcome page shown in Figure 6-9 displays next. Click Database on the left menu.

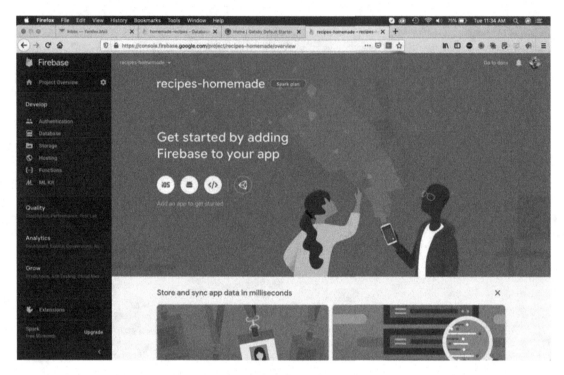

Figure 6-9. *Welcome page*

On the database page, click Create Database . This opens the Create database dialog box shown in Figure 6-10. Click Next.

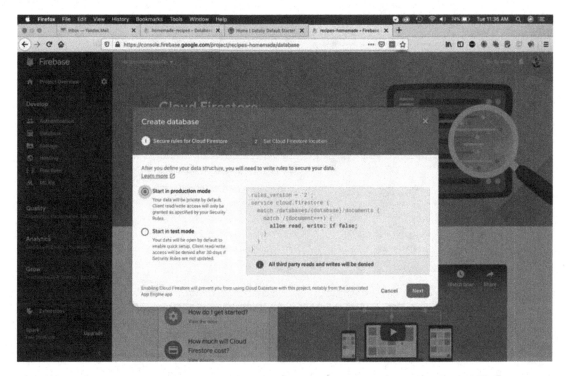

Figure 6-10. *Create database dialog box*

In the next dialog box, you have to select the Firestore location (Figure 6-11). I selected Europe-West, as it is closer to India and will result in less latency. Once you have made your selection, click Done .

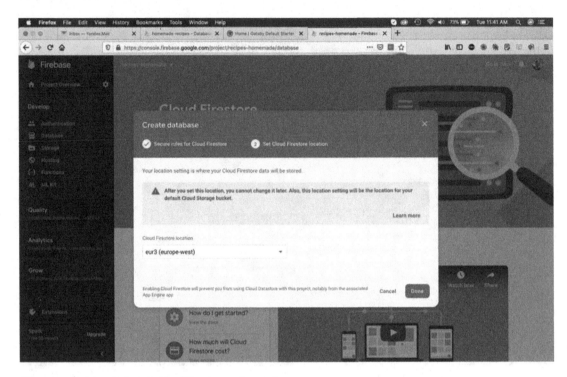

Figure 6-11. *Selecting a Firestore location*

Next, we will be presented with a nice clean database. To begin adding data, click +
Start collection, as shown in Figure 6-12.

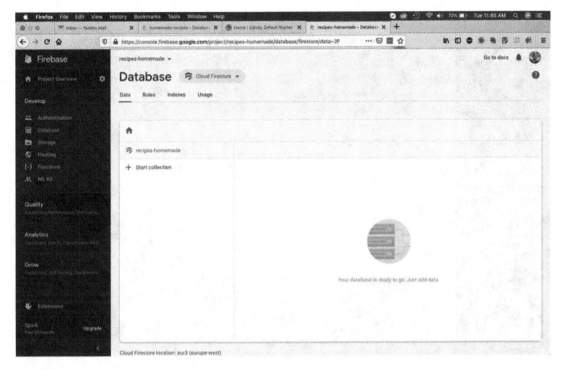

Figure 6-12. *New database*

In the Start a collection dialog box (Figure 6-13), we will give our first collection a name in the Collection ID field, in this case, cooks. After the name is entered, click Next.

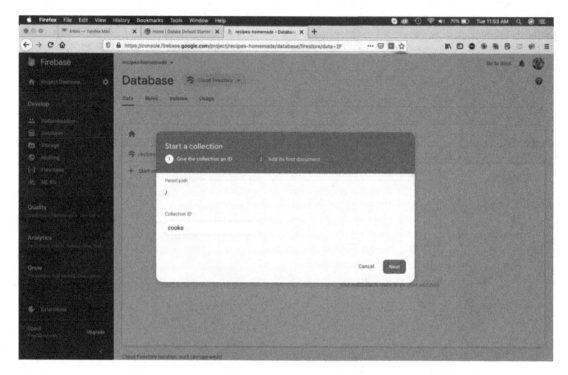

Figure 6-13. *Entering a Collection ID*

Next, give under Field, enter name. Use your name in the Value field. Click Save (Figure 6-14).

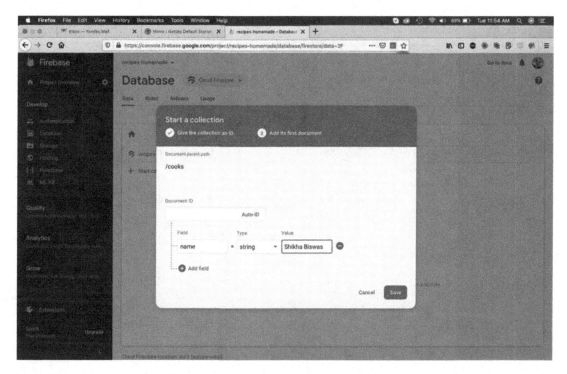

Figure 6-14. *Fields*

Our data will be saved and we will be returned to the Database screen shown in Figure 6-15.

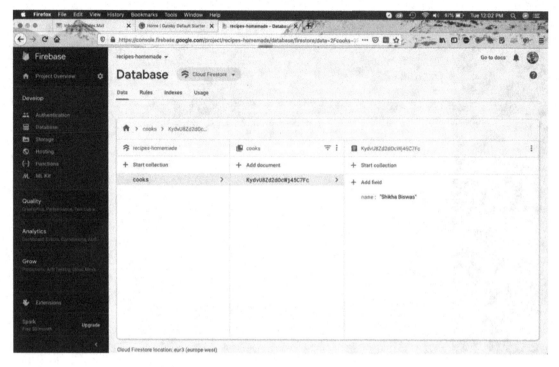

Figure 6-15. *Database screen*

Next, we will add another collection called recipes (Figure 6-16). We are going to reference the cooks collection from it, so copy the cooks ID from the previous screen (KydvU8Zd2dOcWj45C7Fc in this case).

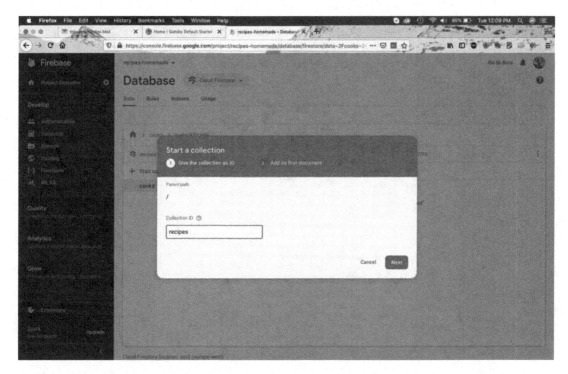

Figure 6-16. *Adding a recipes collection*

Click Next. On the next screen, we will enter names for four fields: name, summary, cook, and link. Now, for in the cook field, from the Type drop-down list, select Reference. Below that, add the cooks ID as the document path (Figure 6-17).

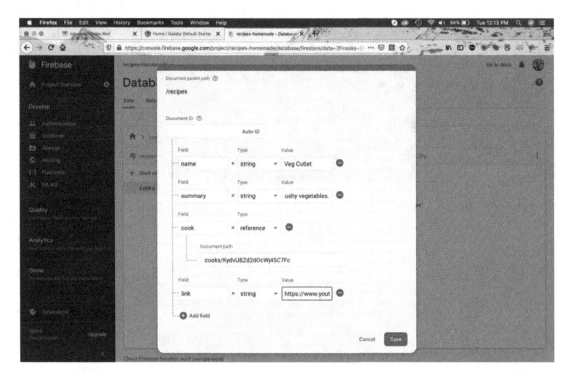

Figure 6-17. *Adding the cooks ID*

Click Save to add the recipes collection. It will be displayed as shown in Figure 6-18.

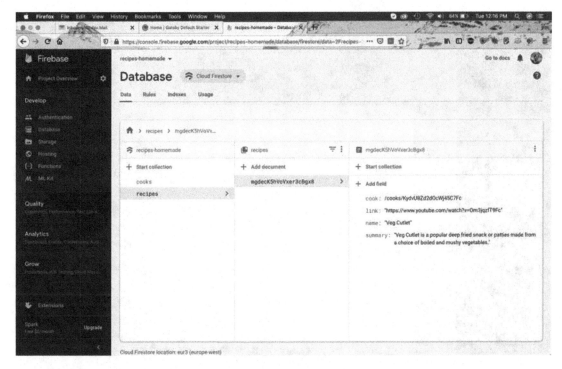

Figure 6-18. *Adding the recipes collection*

Let's add one more document in the recipes collection, by clicking Add document within the recipes collection. (Figure 6-19).

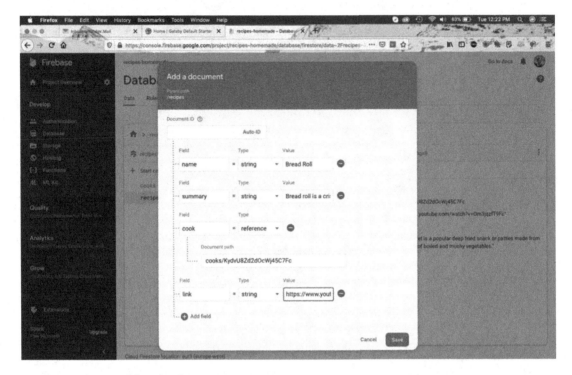

Figure 6-19. *Adding a document*

Now that we've configured Firebase, let's start to connect it to our code.

Completing the Setup

We will be first installing a plug-in to connect Gatsby with firebase called **gatsby-firesource**. Details of the plug-ins are found at `https://www.gatsbyjs.org/packages/gatsby-firesource/?=gatsby-firesource`.

So, head over to the terminal and stop `gatsby develop`, if it is running, and run `npm i gatsby-firesource` to install it.

As usual, we need to add the configuration in the `gatsby-config.js` file, but first we need to get the credential of our Firebase project from the Firebase console. In the console, click on the Settings icon next to Project Overview, then select Project settings (Figure 6-20).

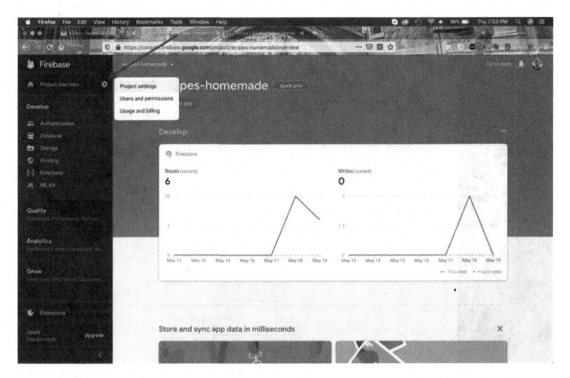

Figure 6-20. *Project settings*

Next, click the Service accounts tab and then click Generate new private key (Figure 6-21).

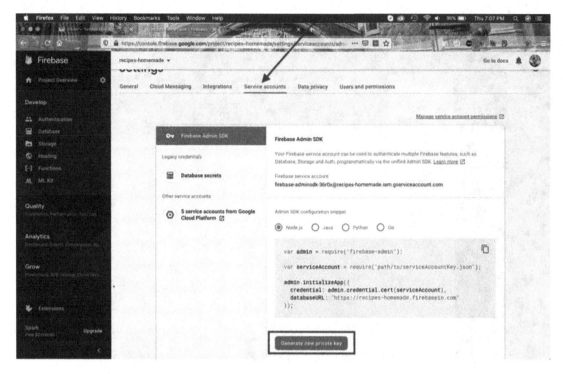

Figure 6-21. *Service accounts*

That will open a pop-up window, where you'll click Generate key. That will save the private key as a JSON file on our local drive (Figure 6-22).

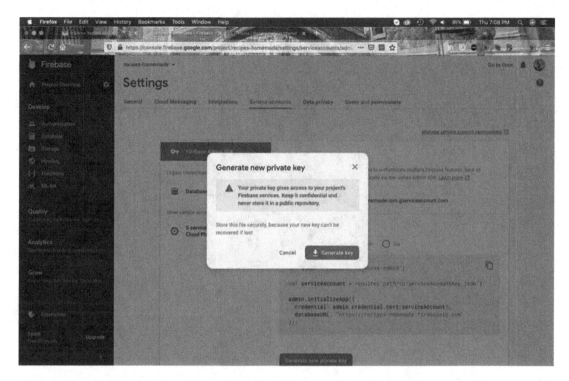

Figure 6-22. *Storing the JSON file*

Rename the downloaded file `firebase.json` and copy it to the root directory of the project (Figure 6-23).

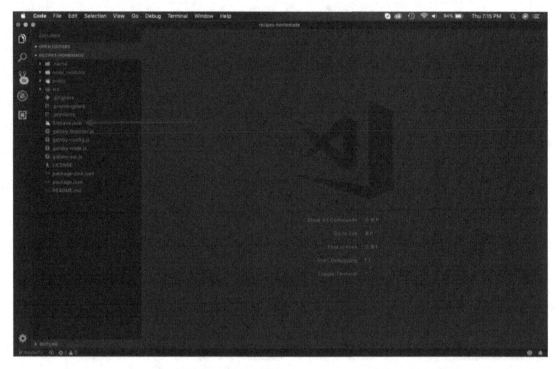

Figure 6-23. `firebase.json`

Now open the `gatsby-config.js` file and add the configuration. Here we are first taking the credentials from the stored `firebase.json` file. After that we are using the collections that we have already saved in the previous part. Notice that cook is using a special format, because it is a reference. The updated content is shown in bold in Listing 6-1.

Listing 6-1. gatsby-config.js

```
module.exports = {
  siteMetadata: {
    title: `Gatsby Default Starter`,
    description: `Kick off your next, great Gatsby project with this
    default starter. This barebones starter ships with the main Gatsby
    configuration files you might need.`,
    author: `@gatsbyjs`,
  },
  plugins: [
...
```

```
...
  `gatsby-transformer-sharp`,
  `gatsby-plugin-sharp`,
  {
    resolve: 'gatsby-firesource',
    options: {
      credential: require('./firebase.json'),
      types: [
        {
          type: 'Recipe',
          collection: 'recipes',
          map: doc => ({
            name: doc.name,
            summary: doc.summary,
            link: doc.link,
            cook___NODE: doc.cook.id
          }),
        },
        {
          type: 'Cook',
          collection: 'cooks',
          map: doc => ({
            name: doc.name,
          }),
        },
      ],
    },
  },
  {
    resolve: `gatsby-plugin-manifest`,
    options: {
      name: `gatsby-starter-default`,
      short_name: `starter`,
      start_url: `/`,
      background_color: `#663399`,
```

```
        theme_color: `#663399`,
        display: `minimal-ui`,
        icon: `src/images/gatsby-icon.png`, // This path is relative to the
                                        root of the site.
    },
   },
 ],
}
```

Next, restart the Gatsby development server by running `gatsby develop` from the terminal. It should run successfully if there are no errors. Now to check if everything is working correctly, we can run the `graphql` query in the playground at `http://localhost:8000/__graphql`, which we will soon use in our code.

The query is returning both of our recipes with all the details successfully (Figure 6-24).

Figure 6-24. *Graphql*

You can find the code for this in the GitHub repo at `https://github.com/nabendu82/recipes-homemade`.

Summary

In this chapter, we have completed the basic setup for Gatsby and Firebase. After that, we created data in the Firebase database and connected it to our Gatsby project. In the next chapter we will display the recipe data on our home page.

CHAPTER 7

Displaying Recipes from Firebase

Now that we have completed the initial setup of our recipe site, it's time to use the graphql in our code so we can display recipes. In this chapter, we will first update the code for our home page. Then we will create the individual pages and change the title and footer. Finally, we will be showing Recipe Details and updating the home page. First, though, we need to remove all the boilerplate code from our Gatsby default starter.

Updating the Code

The first step is to open the index.js file inside the pages folder and update it as shown in Listing 7-1. Notice that we are using the graphql query from the previous chapter here.

Listing 7-1. index.js

```
import React from "react"
import { graphql } from "gatsby"
import Layout from "../components/layout"
import SEO from "../components/seo"

const IndexPage = (props) => {
  console.log(props);
  return (
    <Layout>
      <SEO title="Home" />
    </Layout>
  )
}
```

© Nabendu Biswas 2021
N. Biswas, *Advanced Gatsby Projects*, https://doi.org/10.1007/978-1-4842-6640-3_7

```
export const query = graphql`
  {
    allRecipe {
      edges {
        node {
          id
          link
          name
          summary
            cook {
              name
            }
        }
      }
    }
  }
`;
```

```
export default IndexPage
```

Now, in your browser, head over to `http://localhost:8000/` and open the developer tools. There, as shown in Figure 7-1, you can can see that we are receiving the object containing our two recipes back from Firebase.

Figure 7-1. *localhost*

Next, let's update our `index.js` file to show these data on our home page. We are just looping through the data received from Firebase and displaying it. The updated code is shown in bold in Listing 7-2.

Listing 7-2. `index.js` showing these data on our home page

```
...
...

const IndexPage = (props) => {
  console.log(props);
  return (
    <Layout>
      <SEO title="Home" />
      {props.data.allRecipe.edges.map(edge => (
          <div key={edge.node.id}>
            <h2>{edge.node.name} - <small>{edge.node.cook.name}</small>
            </h2>
```

```
            <div>{edge.node.summary}</div>
            <div>{edge.node.link}</div>
        </div>
      ))}
  </Layout>
  )
}

...

...
```

It will now show our recipes, but with no styling, as they appear in Figure 7-2. We will style them a bit later.

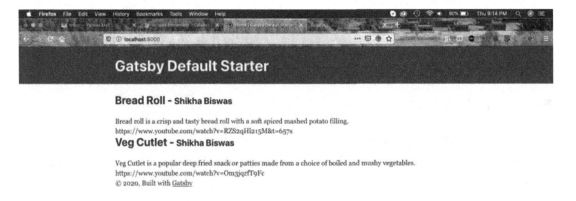

Figure 7-2. *Initial home page*

Now, we want to show individual pages also. To show them we need to generate pages dynamically.

Creating Individual Pages

Navigate to `gatsby-node.js` and add the code given in Listing 7-3 to the file. This is used to create pages and is Node JS code. Here, we are querying our `graphql` query, which returns a promise. We are then checking for errors and if no errors are there, we are looping through the result and creating pages. The path of each page will contain the unique node ID.

Listing 7-3. `gatsby-node.js`

```
exports.createPages = ({graphql, actions}) => {
  const {createPage} = actions;

  return graphql(`
  {
    allRecipe {
      edges {
        node {
          id
          link
          name
          summary
            cook {
              name
            }
        }
      }
    }
  }`).then(result => {
      if(result.errors){
          throw result.errors;
      }

      result.data.allRecipe.edges.forEach(recipe =>{
          createPage({
              path: `/recipe/${recipe.node.id}`,
              component: null,
              context: recipe.node
          })
      });
  })
}
```

Next, we will make a react component to be shown, in place of null. Create a folder named templates inside src and add a file named recipeTemplate.js inside that folder. Put a basic functional component inside it for now, as given in Listing 7-4.

Listing 7-4. recipeTemplate.js with a functional component

```
import React from 'react'

const RecipeTemplate = () => {
  return (
    <div>
      Recipe Page
    </div>
  )
}

export default RecipeTemplate
```

Now, let's update the file gatsby-node.js to use this RecipeTemplate component. The updated code is shown in bold in Listing 7-5.

Listing 7-5. gatsby-node.js with RecipeTemplate component

```
const path = require('path');

exports.createPages = ({graphql, actions}) => {
  const {createPage} = actions;
  const recipeTemplate = path.resolve('src/templates/recipeTemplate.js');

  return graphql(`
  {
  ...
  ...
  }`).then(result => {
      if(result.errors){
          throw result.errors;
      }
```

```
    result.data.allRecipe.edges.forEach(recipe =>{
        createPage({
            path: `/recipe/${recipe.node.id}`,
            component: recipeTemplate,
            context: recipe.node
        })
    });
  })
}
```

Now, let's add a link to the index.js file to show the two pages that we have right now. The updated code is shown in bold in Listing 7-6.

Listing 7-6. Adding a link to index.js

```
import React from "react"
import { Link, graphql } from "gatsby"
import Layout from "../components/layout"
import SEO from "../components/seo"

const IndexPage = (props) => {
  console.log(props);
  return (
    <Layout>
      <SEO title="Home" />
      {props.data.allRecipe.edges.map(edge => (
          <div key={edge.node.id}>
            <h2>{edge.node.name} - <small>{edge.node.cook.name}</small>
            </h2>
            <div>{edge.node.summary}</div>
            <div>{edge.node.link}</div>
            <Link to={`/recipe/${edge.node.id}`}>Comment</Link>
          </div>
      ))}
    </Layout>
  )
}
```

Now, our home page will show two links, as displayed in Figure 7-3.

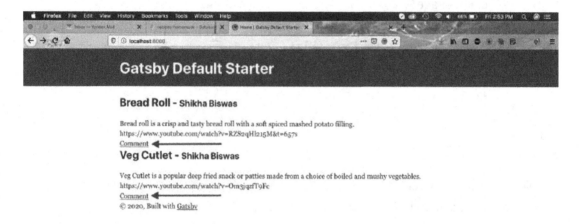

Figure 7-3. *Comment links*

Now, both of our pages will be shown once we click on the respective Comment link (Figures 7-4 and 7-5). Also notice that each will have a different /recipe/id.

Figure 7-4. *Page 1*

Figure 7-5. *Page 2*

Changing the Title and Footer

Before moving forward, let's change our site title. Open the file gatsby-config.js and change the title, description, and author settings. The updated code is shown in bold in Listing 7-7.

Listing 7-7. Modifying `gatsby-config.js`

```
module.exports = {
  siteMetadata: {
    title: `Recipes Homemade`,
    description: `This site contains details of homemade recipes made by
    Shikha Biswas.`,
    author: `Nabendu Biswas`,
  },
  plugins: [
    ],
}
```

Restart `gatsby develop` for the changes to take effect (Figure 7-6).

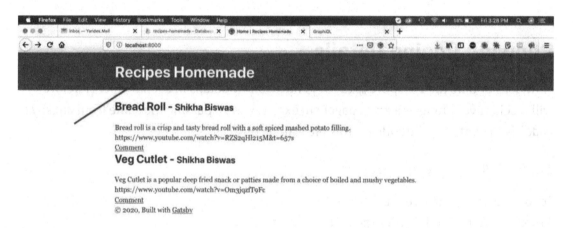

Figure 7-6. *Title changed*

Let's also change the footer of each page by changing it in the `Layout.js` file. The updated code is shown in bold in Listing 7-8.

Listing 7-8. `Layout.js`

```
    ...
    ...
    <main>{children}</main>
    <footer style={{
      marginTop: `2rem`
```

```
      }}>
        © {new Date().getFullYear()}, Built with
        {` `}
        <a href="https://thewebdev.tech">Nabendu Biswas</a>
      </footer>
    </div>

  )
}

Layout.propTypes = {
  children: PropTypes.node.isRequired,
}

export default Layout
```

Showing Recipe Details

Now, let's update the recipeTemplate.js file to show details of each recipe. Here, we will receive everything as a prop, pageContext, as we are passing the same from gatsby-node.js in context. The code for this file is in Listing 7-9.

Listing 7-9. recipeTemplate.js

```
import React from 'react'
import Layout from '../components/layout'

const RecipeTemplate = ({ pageContext }) => {
  return (
    <Layout>
      <section>
          <h2>{pageContext.name} - <small>{pageContext.cook.name}</small>
          </h2>
          <p>{pageContext.summary}</p>
          <p>{pageContext.link}</p>
      </section>
```

```
    </Layout>
  )
}

export default RecipeTemplate
```

Now, when we go to any recipe page, it will display as shown in Figure 7-7.

Figure 7-7. *Initial recipe page*

We will use `styled-components` in this project, so we will install the Gatsby plug-in for the same. Details of the plug-in can be found at `https://www.gatsbyjs.org/packages/gatsby-plugin-styled-components/?=styled`. As per the documentation, we have to `npm install` the following packages:

```
npm install --save gatsby-plugin-styled-components styled-components babel-plugin-styled-components
```

Stop `gatsby develop` and install the packages. Next, we will add the plug-in in the `gatsby-config.js` file. The updated code is shown in bold in Listing 7-10.

Listing 7-10. Adding a plug-in to `gatsby-config.js`

```
module.exports = {
  siteMetadata: {
  ...
  ...
  },
  plugins: [
    `gatsby-plugin-react-helmet`,
```

```
`gatsby-plugin-styled-components`,
{
  resolve: `gatsby-source-filesystem`,
  options: {
    name: `images`,
    path: `${__dirname}/src/images`,
  },
},
...
...
],
}
```

Next, rerun **gatsby develop** to use styled-components in our project.

It's time to update the RecipeTemplate component to perfect our display. Let's update the recipeTemplate.js file. Here, we are wrapping everything in a RecipeItemWrapper component, which is a styled component. We have also created a new Link, which will take us back to all recipes.

Next, let's write the styled components now. Here, we are first importing styled-components and Link, which is required in the file. After that we are writing the style for RecipeItemWrapper. Now, in the styled component we can write the styles for all classes that come inside it. We are therefore writing styles for the link class, which will render a button.

Now, let's add some more styles for the info class, which is wrapping all of our content. The updated code is shown in bold in Listing 7-11.

Listing 7-11. Adding more styles for info class

```
import React from 'react'
import styled from 'styled-components';
import { Link } from "gatsby"

const RecipeItemWrapper = styled.section`
    width: 100vw;
    margin: 4rem auto;
    padding: 2rem;
```

```css
.link {
    border: 1px solid black;
    padding: 4px 8px;
    display: inline-block;
    color: black;
    text-decoration: none;
    text-transform: capitalize;
    transition: all 0.3s ease-in-out;
    margin-bottom: 2rem;

    &:hover{
        background: black;
        color: white;
    }
  }
.info {
    text-align: center;
    margin-bottom: 1rem;
}

.info h1 {
    letter-spacing: 5px;
    margin-bottom: 0.5rem;
    text-transform: capitalize;
    font-size: 48px;
}

.info h4 {
    letter-spacing: 5px;
    text-transform: capitalize;
    font-size: 14px;
    text-align: center;
    margin-bottom: 0.5rem;
}
```

```
  .info p{
      margin: 0.95em 0 1.2em;
      padding: 0.2em;
  }
`;

const RecipeTemplate = ({ pageContext }) => {
  return (
    <RecipeItemWrapper>
      <Link to="/" className="link">back to all recipes</Link>
      <div className="info">
          <h1>{pageContext.name}</h1>
          <h4>{pageContext.cook.name}</h4>
          <p>{pageContext.summary}</p>
          <a href={pageContext.link} target="_blank" rel="noopener
          noreferrer" className="link">
            Youtube
          </a>
      </div>
    </RecipeItemWrapper>
  )
}

export default RecipeTemplate
```

Now, our individual recipe page will look like Figure 7-8.

Figure 7-8. *Recipe page with components added*

We need to update our home page to show each recipe on a nice card. Before that, though, let's update our layout.js file. The updated code is shown in bold in Listing 7-12.

Listing 7-12. Updating layout.js

```
...
...

  return (

      <Header siteTitle={data.site.siteMetadata?.title || `Title`} />
        <main>{children}</main>
        <footer style={{ textAlign: 'center' }}>
          © {new Date().getFullYear()}, Built by
          {` `}
          <a href="https://thewebdev.tech">Nabendu Biswas</a>
        </footer>
    </>
  )
}

Layout.propTypes = {
  children: PropTypes.node.isRequired,
}

export default Layout
```

We will also remove the default content of the layout.css file and use our own styles. The code for these styles is given in Listing 7-13.

Listing 7-13. layout.css

```
@import url("https://fonts.googleapis.com/css?family=Quicksand&display=swap");

* {
    box-sizing: border-box;
    margin: 0;
}
```

```css
:root {
    --mainGrey: #F9F9FA;
    --mainBlack: #0A0A0A;
    --mainTransition: all 0.3s linear;
    --mainSpacing: 4px;
}

body {
    font-family: "Quicksand", sans-serif;
    background: var(--mainGrey);
    color: var(--mainBlack);
    font-size: 18px;
    overflow-x: hidden;
}
```

Updating the Home Page

Now, let's update our home page in `index.js` to show each recipe on a card. We are wrapping everything in an `AllRecipes` `styled-component`. The updated code is shown in bold in Listing 7-14.

Listing 7-14. Showing each recipe on a card

```js
import SEO from "../components/seo"
import styled from 'styled-components';

const AllRecipes = styled.section`
  padding: 1rem 0;
  width: 85vw;
  margin: 0 auto;
  max-width: 730px;
  .card {
    box-shadow: 2px 2px 6px 0px rgba(142,142,142,1);
    border: none;
    border-radius: 4px;
    outline: none;
```

228

```
      margin-bottom: 2rem;
      background: white;
      padding: 1rem;
      text-align: center;
  }
`;

const IndexPage = (props) => {
  return (
    <Layout>
      <SEO title="Home" />
      <AllRecipes>
        {props.data.allRecipe.edges.map(edge => (
            <article className="card" key={edge.node.id}>
              <h2>{edge.node.name} - <small>{edge.node.cook.name}</small>
              </h2>
              <div>{edge.node.summary}</div>
              <div>{edge.node.link}</div>
              <Link to={`/recipe/${edge.node.id}`}>Comment</Link>
            </article>
        ))}
      </AllRecipes>
    </Layout>
  )
}
```

Now, our home page, displayed in Figure 7-9, is showing nice cards.

Figure 7-9. *Home page with cards*

Now, let's wrap all the content in an `info` class `div` and write styles for it. We will also update the styles for the `Link`, to show it as a button. The updated code is shown in bold in Listing 7-15.

Listing 7-15. Wrapping all the content in an `info` class `div`

```
...
...

const AllRecipes = styled.section`
  padding: 1rem 0;
  width: 85vw;
  margin: 0 auto;
  max-width: 730px;
  .card {
    box-shadow: 2px 2px 6px 0px rgba(142,142,142,1);
    border: none;
    border-radius: 4px;
    outline: none;
    margin-bottom: 2rem;
    background: white;
```

```
    padding: 1rem;
    text-align: center;
  }
  .info {
    padding: 1rem 0;
  }
  .info h2 {
      font-size: 30px;
      text-transform: capitalize;
      margin-bottom: 10px;
  }
  .info h5 {
      color: var(--darkGrey);
      text-transform: capitalize;
  }
  .info p {
      padding: 20px 0 30px 0;
      text-align: left;
  }
  .link {
    border: 1px solid black;
    padding: 4px 8px;
    display: inline-block;
    color: black;
    text-decoration: none;
    text-transform: capitalize;
    transition: all 0.3s ease-in-out;

    &:hover{
        background: black;
        color: white;
    }
  }
}
`;
```

```
const IndexPage = (props) => {
  return (
    <Layout>
      <SEO title="Home" />
      <AllRecipes>
        {props.data.allRecipe.edges.map(edge => (
            <article className="card" key={edge.node.id}>
            <div className="info">
              <h2>{edge.node.name}</h2>
              <h5>{edge.node.cook.name}</h5>
              <p>{edge.node.summary}</p>
              <Link to={`/recipe/${edge.node.id}`} className="link">read
              more</Link>
            </div>
            </article>
        ))}
      </AllRecipes>
    </Layout>
  )
}
```

Now, our home page will look like Figure 7-10.

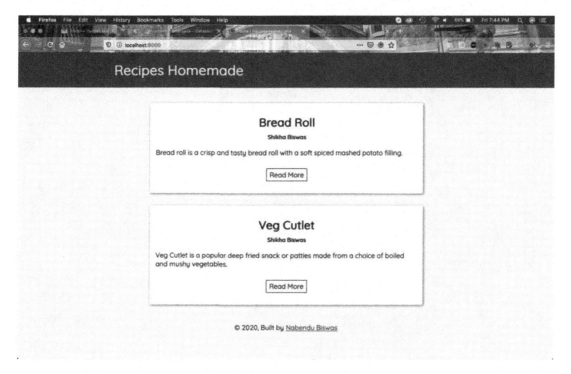

Figure 7-10. *Completed home page*

Summary

In this chapter, we have displayed the recipe data on our home page, as well as a detailed view page. In the next chapter, we will add images in the Firebase database and also display them on our site.

CHAPTER 8

Displaying Images from Firebase

In the previous chapter, we displayed the recipe data on our home page, as well as a detailed view page. In this chapter we will see how to display images using Firebase by following these steps:

1. Store the images in a Firebase database.

2. Add the images in collections within the Firebase database.

3. Optimize images using `gatsby-image`.

4. Show images on different pages.

Storing Images in Firebase

Open the Firebase dashboard and click the Storage tab (Figure 8-1). On the Storage tab, click Get started.

© Nabendu Biswas 2021
N. Biswas, *Advanced Gatsby Projects*, https://doi.org/10.1007/978-1-4842-6640-3_8

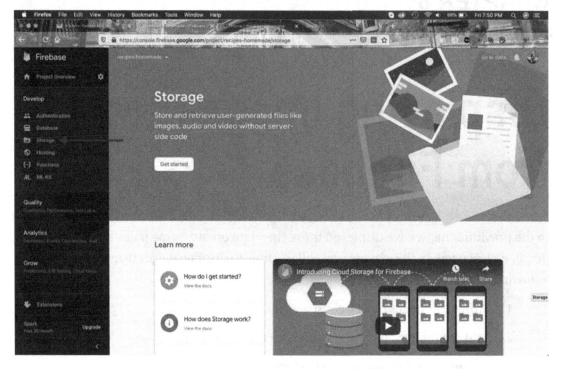

Figure 8-1. *Storage tab*

It will show a pop-up for rules. We will keep the defaults and simply click Next (Figure 8-2).

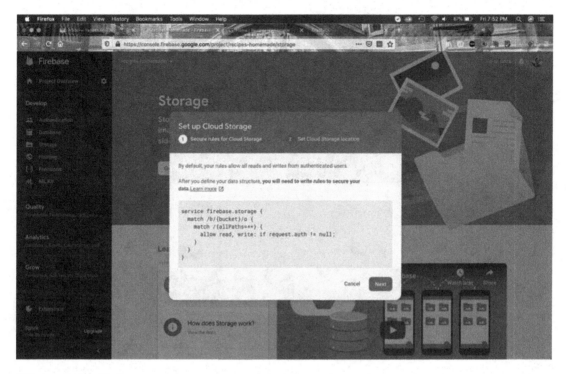

Figure 8-2. *Rules*

In the next pop-up, we need to select the cloud storage location. It is set up to use the default eur3 (Europe-west) region, which we chose during project creation. To retain this setting, simply click Done (Figure 8-3).

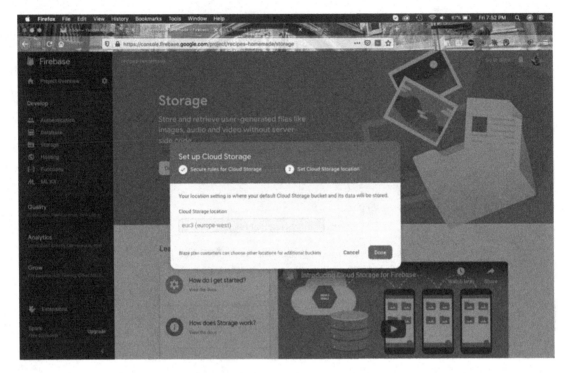

Figure 8-3. *Setting cloud storage location*

Now, on the next screen, click Upload file. After that I will select all the original images of the recipes made by my wife (Figure 8-4).

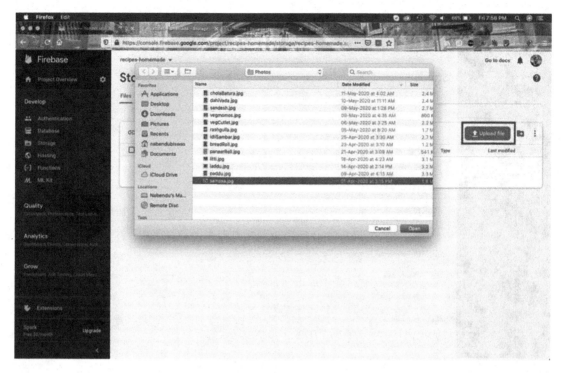

Figure 8-4. *Original recipe images*

Firebase will start uploading them (see Figure 8-5), but it will take some time.

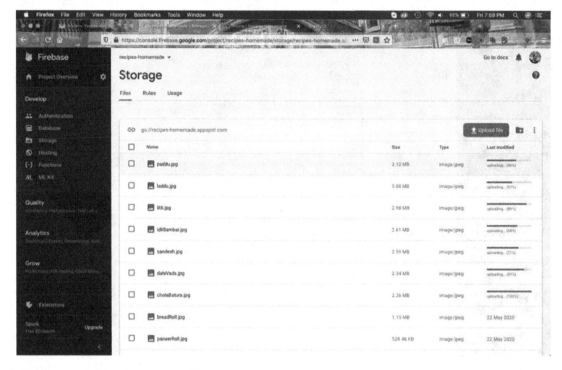

Figure 8-5. *Images uploading*

Now that we have stored all our images in Firebase, it's time to add them in our collections.

Adding the Images in Collections

After uploading images to storage inside Firebase in the previous section, we will add the links for these images in our collections. The link is required for us to use it in our code.

So, head over to storage and click the name of the image you want to add. This will open the image in a new tab, from which you can copy the whole address (Figure 8-6).

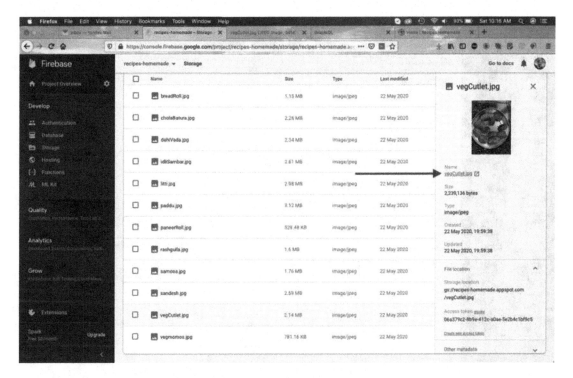

Figure 8-6. *Adding an image to storage*

After that, click the Database tab and then the document in which you want to place the image. Add a new string field called `imageUrl`, and then paste the image address from the preceding step into this field. Repeat this process for all other recipes (Figure 8-7).

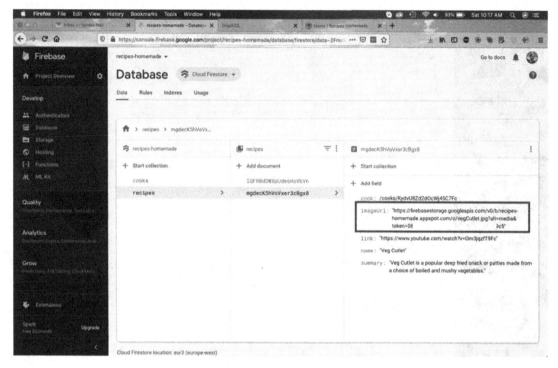

Figure 8-7. *Adding fields on the Database tab*

Because we have added a new field, we need to add the same in our `gatsby-config.js` file. The new content for this file is shown in bold in Listing 8-1.

Listing 8-1. Adding `imageUrl` in `gatsby-config.js`

```
module.exports = {
  siteMetadata: {
  ...
  },
  plugins: [
  ...
  ...
    `gatsby-transformer-sharp`,
    `gatsby-plugin-sharp`,
    {
      resolve: 'gatsby-firesource',
      options: {
```

```
      credential: require('./firebase.json'),
      types: [
        {
          type: 'Recipe',
          collection: 'recipes',
          map: doc => ({
            name: doc.name,
            summary: doc.summary,
            link: doc.link,
            imageUrl: doc.imageUrl,
            cook___NODE: doc.cook.id
          }),
        },
        {
          type: 'Cook',
          collection: 'cooks',
          map: doc => ({
            name: doc.name,
          }),
        },
      ],
    },
  },
  ...
  ...
  ],
}
```

Because we have made changes in the gatsby-config.js file, we need to restart gatsby develop in the terminal.

In the next step, we'll set up the image to display on our home page. Open the index.js file and first add imageUrl in our graphql query. After that, add a new div containing the image.

Now, we will style the image. So, inside our styled component at the end, add the below code shown in bold in Listing 8-2. Here, we are also adding a media query for desktop screens, where we are dividing the space with help of grid as 250px and 1fr. The 250px is for the image and the rest of the space is for the content.

Listing 8-2. Adding images and styles in index.js

```
const AllRecipes = styled.section`
...
...
  .link {
    border: 1px solid black;
    padding: 4px 8px;
    display: inline-block;
    color: black;
    text-decoration: none;
    text-transform: capitalize;
    transition: all 0.3s ease-in-out;

    &:hover{
        background: black;
        color: white;
    }
  }
  .image{
    max-width: 360px;
    img{
      max-width: 360px;
    }
  }
  @media (min-width: 776px){
    .card {
      display: grid;
      grid-template-columns: 250px 1fr;
      box-shadow: 2px 2px 6px 0px rgba(142,142,142,1);
      border: none;
      border-radius: 4px;
```

```
      outline: none;
      margin-bottom: 2rem;
      background: white;
      padding: 1rem;
      text-align: center;
    }
    .info {
      display: flex;
      flex-direction: column;
      align-items: center;
      padding: 0 1.5rem;
    }
    .image {
      max-width: 200px;
      img{
        max-width: 200px;
      }
    }
  }
`;

const IndexPage = (props) => {
  return (
    <Layout>
      <SEO title="Home" />
      <AllRecipes>
        {props.data.allRecipe.edges.map(edge => (
            <article className="card" key={edge.node.id}>
            <div className="image">
              <img src={edge.node.imageUrl} alt="recipe image" />
            </div>
            <div className="info">
            ...
            ...
            </div>
            </article>
```

```
        ))}
      </AllRecipes>
    </Layout>
  )
}

export const query = graphql`
  {
    allRecipe {
      edges {
        node {
          id
          link
          imageUrl
          name
          summary
            cook {
              name
            }
        }
      }
    }
  }
`;

export default IndexPage
```

Now, it will look like Figure 8-8 on desktop screens.

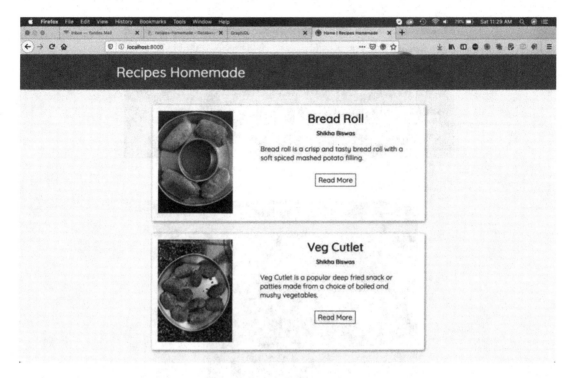

Figure 8-8. *Media query on desktop screens*

Figure 8-9 shows the result on mobile screens.

Figure 8-9. *Media query on a mobile screen*

Let's now show images for each recipe page. For this we also have to add the imageUrl in the gatsby-node.js file. After this we need to restart gatsby develop running on the terminal. The updated content for this file is shown in bold in Listing 8-3.

Listing 8-3. Adding imageUrl in gatsby-node.js

```
const path = require('path');

exports.createPages = ({graphql, actions}) => {
...

...

  return graphql(`
  {
    allRecipe {
      edges {
        node {
          id
          link
          name
          imageUrl
          summary
            cook {
              name
            }
        }
      }
    }
  }`).then(result => {
  ...
  ...
  })
}
```

Now in the recipeTemplate.js file, we have the imageUrl available in pageContext. We are therefore displaying it with a little bit of help from CSS. The updated content for this file is shown in bold in Listing 8-4.

Listing 8-4. Adding imageUrl in recipeTemplate.js

```
...

const RecipeItemWrapper = styled.section`
...
...

  .info p{
      margin: 0.95em 0 1.2em;
      padding: 0.2em;
  }

  img {
    max-width: 400px;
  }
`;

const RecipeTemplate = ({ pageContext }) => {
  return (
    <RecipeItemWrapper>
      <Link to="/" className="link">back to all recipes</Link>
      <div className="info">
          <h1>{pageContext.name}</h1>
          <h4>{pageContext.cook.name}</h4>
          <img src={pageContext.imageUrl} alt="recipe image" />
          <p>{pageContext.summary}</p>
          <a href={pageContext.link} target="_blank" rel="noopener
          noreferrer" className="link">
            Youtube
          </a>
      </div>
    </RecipeItemWrapper>
  )
}

export default RecipeTemplate
```

It will appear as shown in Figure 8-10 on desktop screens.

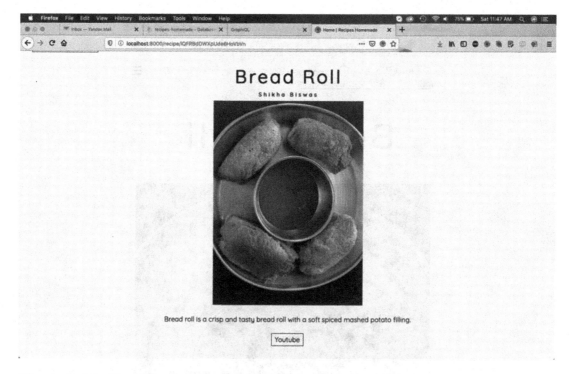

Figure 8-10. *YouTube link shown on desktop screens*

It will look like Figure 8-11 on mobile screens.

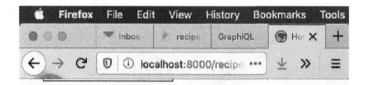

Figure 8-11. *YouTube link shown on mobile screens*

Although images are displayed in our project, this is not the best way to display them in Gatsby. The images are stored as URLs in the Firebase database and we are taking it from there. It slows down the site, especially in the case of a larger site. We will optimize that in the next section, using `gatsby-image`, a React component specially designed to work seamlessly with Gatsby's GraphQL queries.

Using `gatsby-image`

We will be using `gatsby-image` to display images in Gatsby, which downloads the images from Firebase and makes them a part of our static site.

We will convert our code to use the optimized `gatsby-image` now. For any site, the loading of images takes most of the time and it can slow down the site. For our site this is also the case, and we will fix it using `gatsby-image`.

We will be using `gatsby-plugin-remote-images` for this. The relevant documentation can be found at `https://www.gatsbyjs.org/packages/gatsby-plugin-remote-images/?=remote%20im`.

First we need to install it using the following npm command. Stop `gatsby develop` and run this command on the terminal.

```
npm install --save gatsby-plugin-remote-images
```

Now, we need to add the plug-in in our `gatsby-config.js` file. The updated content to do so is shown in bold in Listing 8-5.

Listing 8-5. Adding the Gatsby remote images plug-in in `gatsby-config.js`

```
module.exports = {
...
...
  plugins: [
  ...
  ...
    {
      resolve: `gatsby-plugin-manifest`,
      options: {
        name: `gatsby-starter-default`,
        short_name: `starter`,
```

```
        start_url: `/`,
        background_color: `#663399`,
        theme_color: `#663399`,
        display: `minimal-ui`,
        icon: `src/images/gatsby-icon.png`, // This path is relative to the
                                            root of the site.
      },
    },
    {
      resolve: `gatsby-plugin-remote-images`,
      options: {
        nodeType: 'Recipe',
        imagePath: 'imageUrl',
      },
    }
  ],
}
```

Now, we can start gatsby develop on the terminal. After that, let's check the way we will get this image in our graphql query. We are getting the image in localImage and from there, we will get it through Gatsby's childImageSharp. Because we are displaying the image on both desktop and mobile sites, we are using the fluid property (Figure 8-12).

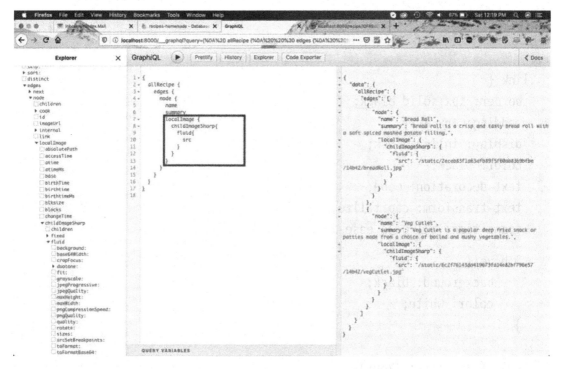

Figure 8-12. *Graphql*

Now, we will use this to display images. So, in `index.js` first put the import for `gatsby-image` at the top. After that, let's replace the `imageUrl` in the `graphql` query with the `localImage` query. Also, notice that instead of `src` we have to use `...GatsbyImageSharpFluid_withWebp` in our query.

After that, we are using the new `Image` tag from Gatsby and pass the `localImage` as props `fluid`.

We also need to update the style a bit, because our image is fluid. We are just targeting the `div` within the image and setting it to `250px`. The updated content for the file is shown in bold in Listing 8-6.

Listing 8-6. Using local images from `gatsby-image` in `index.js`

```
...
...
import styled from 'styled-components';
import Image from "gatsby-image";
```

```
const AllRecipes = styled.section`
...
...
  .link {
    border: 1px solid black;
    padding: 4px 8px;
    display: inline-block;
    color: black;
    text-decoration: none;
    text-transform: capitalize;
    transition: all 0.3s ease-in-out;

    &:hover{
        background: black;
        color: white;
    }
  }
  @media (min-width: 776px){
    .card {
      display: grid;
      grid-template-columns: 250px 1fr;
      box-shadow: 2px 2px 6px 0px rgba(142,142,142,1);
      border: none;
      border-radius: 4px;
      outline: none;
      margin-bottom: 2rem;
      background: white;
      padding: 1rem;
      text-align: center;
    }
    .info {
      display: flex;
      flex-direction: column;
      align-items: center;
      padding: 0 1.5rem;
    }
```

```
    .image > div {
      height: 250px;
    }
  }
`;

const IndexPage = (props) => {
  return (
    <Layout>
      <SEO title="Home" />
      <AllRecipes>
        {props.data.allRecipe.edges.map(edge => (
          <article className="card" key={edge.node.id}>
          <div className="image">
            <Image fluid={edge.node.localImage.childImageSharp.fluid} />
          </div>
          <div className="info">
          ...
          ...
          </div>
          </article>
        ))}
      </AllRecipes>
    </Layout>
  )
}

export const query = graphql`
  {
    allRecipe {
      edges {
        node {
          id
          link
```

```
        localImage {
          childImageSharp{
            fluid{
              ...GatsbyImageSharpFluid_withWebp
            }
          }
        }
        name
        summary
          cook {
            name
          }
      }
    }
  }
}
`;

export default IndexPage
```

Now our home page is looking great in the desktop view and it is also loading fast. We were targeting the `div` in the preceding styles, because `gatsby-image` creates a `div` to wrap the image (Figure 8-13).

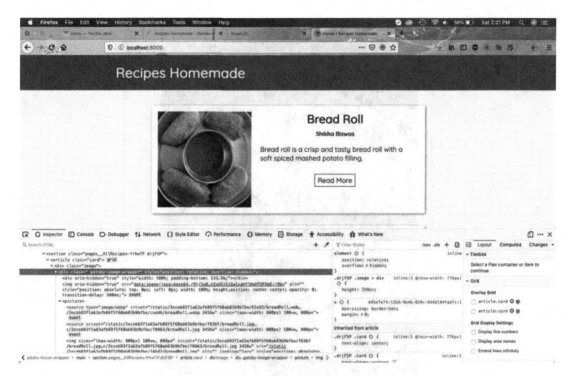

Figure 8-13. *Updated desktop view of the home page*

It will look like Figure 8-14 in the mobile view.

Figure 8-14. *Updated mobile screen view of home page*

Let's change the imageUrl in gatsby-node.js with localImage as in index.js. Also, don't forget to rerun gatsby develop after that. The updated content for the file is shown in bold in Listing 8-7.

Listing 8-7. Changing imageUrl in gatsby-node.js

```
const path = require('path');

exports.createPages = ({graphql, actions}) => {
  const {createPage} = actions;
  const recipeTemplate = path.resolve('src/templates/recipeTemplate.js');

  return graphql(`
  {
    allRecipe {
      edges {
        node {
          id
          link
          name
          localImage {
            childImageSharp{
              fluid{
                ...GatsbyImageSharpFluid_withWebp
              }
            }
          }
          summary
            cook {
              name
            }
        }
      }
    }
  }`).then(result => {
```

```
...
...
})
}
```

Now, if we go to any recipe page our terminal will throw the error shown in Listing 8-8 and the page will also not load.

Listing 8-8. Terminal error

```
"gatsby-node.js" threw an error while running the createPages lifecycle:
Unknown fragment "GatsbyImageSharpFluid_withWebp".
  GraphQLError: Unknown fragment "GatsbyImageSharpFluid_withWebp".
```

The reason is that we cannot use fragments like ...GatsbyImageSharpFluid_ withWebp in graphql query inside the gatsby-node.js file. Therefore, to show the image inside each recipe page, we have to modify our logic a bit.

Showing Images Inside Pages

We will delete everything from graphql query in gatsby-node.js and will pass only the id, as recipeId in the context variable. The updated content for the file is shown in bold in Listing 8-9.

Listing 8-9. Passing id from gatsby-node.js

```
const path = require('path');

exports.createPages = ({graphql, actions}) => {
  const {createPage} = actions;
  const recipeTemplate = path.resolve('src/templates/recipeTemplate.js');

  return graphql(`
  {
    allRecipe {
      edges {
        node {
          id
        }
```

```
        }
    }
}`).then(result => {
    if(result.errors){
        throw result.errors;
    }

    result.data.allRecipe.edges.forEach(recipe =>{
        createPage({
            path: `/recipe/${recipe.node.id}`,
            component: recipeTemplate,
            context: { recipeId: recipe.node.id }
        })
    });
})
}
```

Now, in `recipeTemplate.js` we will use a new `graphql` query, which will use the `recipeId` and return all the fields of this single recipe.

Also, at the beginning of the file, update `gatsby import` to include `graphql`. We need to import `Image` from `gatsby-image` at the start of the file. We have also removed the `img` styles from the `RecipeItemWrapper styled-component`. Now, we will be receiving everything as data props. We therefore need to update the same in the `recipeTemplate.js` file. The updated content for this file is shown in bold in Listing 8-10.

Listing 8-10. Using new `RecipeQuery` in `recipeTemplate.js`

```
import React from 'react'
import styled from 'styled-components';
import { graphql, Link } from "gatsby"
import Image from "gatsby-image";

const RecipeItemWrapper = styled.section`
...

...
```

```
  .info h4 {
      letter-spacing: 5px;
      text-transform: capitalize;
      font-size: 14px;
      text-align: center;
      margin-bottom: 0.5rem;
  }

  .info p{
      margin: 0.95em 0 1.2em;
      padding: 0.2em;
  }
`;

const RecipeTemplate = ({ data }) => {
  return (
    <RecipeItemWrapper>
      <Link to="/" className="link">back to all recipes</Link>
      <div className="info">
          <h1>{data.recipe.name}</h1>
          <h4>{data.recipe.cook.name}</h4>
          <Image fluid={data.recipe.localImage.childImageSharp.fluid} />
          <p>{data.recipe.summary}</p>
          <a href={data.recipe.link} target="_blank" rel="noopener
          noreferrer" className="link">
            Youtube
          </a>
      </div>
    </RecipeItemWrapper>
  )
}
```

```
export const query = graphql`
    query RecipeQuery($recipeId: String!) {
        recipe(id: {eq: $recipeId}){
        id
        summary
        name
        link
        localImage{
            childImageSharp{
                fluid{
                   ...GatsbyImageSharpFluid_withWebp
                }
            }
        }
        cook {
                id
                name
            }
        }
    }
`;

export default RecipeTemplate
```

Now, we will receive the large original image, which will change according to screen size (Figure 8-15).

Veg Cutlet is a popular deep fried snack or patties made from a choice of boiled and mushy vegetables.

Figure 8-15. *Fluid image*

Summary

In this chapter, we added images in the Firebase database and also displayed them on our site. In the next chapter, we will deploy our site to Netlify.

CHAPTER 9

Deploying the Recipe Site in Netlify

In the previous chapter, we added images in the Firebase database and learned to use them in our project using `gatsby-image`. After that we displayed them on our site. Our project is almost complete and it's time to deploy it in Netlify. Before that, though, we need to create an environment file, so that our Firebase credentials don't end in GitHub.

Creating an Environment File

Open your `firebase.json` file in the root directory (Figure 9-1). We need to copy everything from this file.

© Nabendu Biswas 2021
N. Biswas, *Advanced Gatsby Projects*, https://doi.org/10.1007/978-1-4842-6640-3_9

Figure 9-1. `firebase.json`

Create a file named .env in the root directory and paste everything from the copied firebase.json file into the variables. One thing to notice is that only the FIREBASE_ PRIVATE_KEY value should be within double quotes(""). The content for this file is given in Listing 9-1.

Listing 9-1. .env file

```
FIREBASE_TYPE=service_account
FIREBASE_PROJECT_ID=recipes-xxxxxx
FIREBASE_PRIVATE_KEY_ID=9cf6xxxxxxxxxxxxxxxxxxxxxx
FIREBASE_PRIVATE_KEY="-----BEGIxxxxxxx—END PRIVATE KEY-----\n",
FIREBASE_CLIENT_EMAIL=firebase-xxxxxxx-36r0x@xxxxxxxxxx
FIREBASE_CLIENT_ID=118xxxxxxxxxxx
FIREBASE_AUTH_URI=https://accounts.google.com/o/oauth2/auth
FIREBASE_TOKEN_URI=https://oauth2.googleapis.com/token
FIREBASE_AUTH_PROVIDER_X509_CERT_URL=https://www.googleapis.com/oaut
FIREBASE_CLIENT_X509_CERT_URL=https://www.googleapis.com/xxxxxxxx
```

After that, navigate to gatsby-config.js and add the imports shown at the top of the file to use the .env file. Next, we will change our credential within the gatsby-firesource plug-in to an object and use these variables. Earlier it was directly referencing the firebase.json file. The updated content for the file is shown in bold in Listing 9-2.

Listing 9-2. gatsby-config.js

```
require('dotenv').config({
  path: '.env'
})

module.exports = {
  siteMetadata: {
  ...
  ...
  },
  plugins: [
  ...
  ...
    `gatsby-transformer-sharp`,
    `gatsby-plugin-sharp`,
    {
      resolve: 'gatsby-firesource',
      options: {
        credential: {
          "type": process.env.FIREBASE_TYPE,
          "project_id": process.env.FIREBASE_PROJECT_ID,
          "private_key_id": process.env.FIREBASE_PRIVATE_KEY_ID,
          "private_key": process.env.FIREBASE_PRIVATE_KEY.replace(/\\n/g, '\n'),
          "client_email": process.env.FIREBASE_CLIENT_EMAIL,
          "client_id": process.env.FIREBASE_CLIENT_ID,
          "auth_uri": process.env.FIREBASE_AUTH_URI,
          "token_uri": process.env.FIREBASE_TOKEN_URI,
```

```
  "auth_provider_x509_cert_url": process.env.FIREBASE_AUTH_PROVIDER_X509_
  CERT_URL,
         "client_x509_cert_url": process.env.FIREBASE_CLIENT_X509_CERT_URL
     },
     types: [
     ...
     ...
  ],
}
```

Next, in your .gitignore file add the firebase.json file at the top, so that it is not pushed to GitHub. The .env file is already added in it. The updated content for the .gitignore file is shown in bold in Listing 9-3.

Listing 9-3. .gitignore

```
firebase.json
# Logs
logs
*.log
npm-debug.log*
yarn-debug.log*
yarn-error.log*

...
...
```

Now, restart gatsby develop to check if everything is working fine. In this case it was working fine, so I pushed the code to GitHub.

Deployment Time

Now, we can deploy our site to Netlify. Once we log in to Netlify we will be presented with the screen shown in Figure 9-2. Click New site from Git.

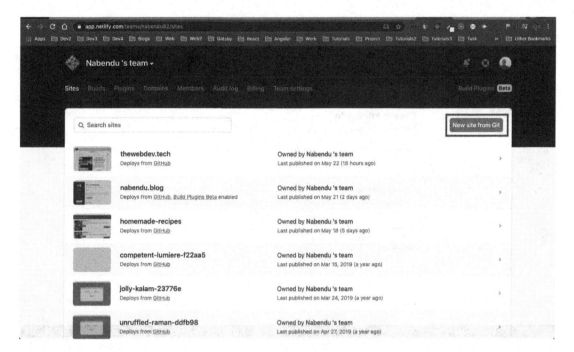

Figure 9-2. *Creating a new site*

On the next screen, displayed in Figure 9-3, I have chosen GitHub, as my site is hosted there.

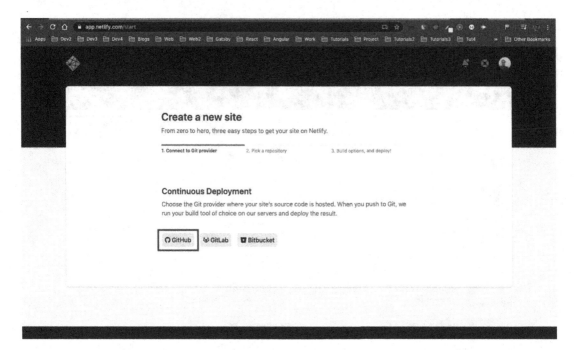

Figure 9-3. *Github*

Next, we need to search the repository in the search box and select it (Figure 9-4).

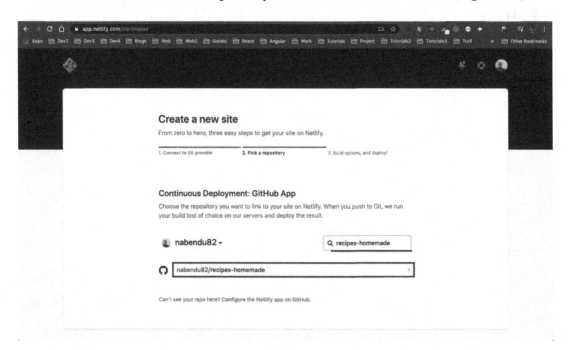

Figure 9-4. *Repo*

On the next screen, we will be shown that the `gatsby build` command will be run on the master branch. Click Deploy site (Figure 9-5).

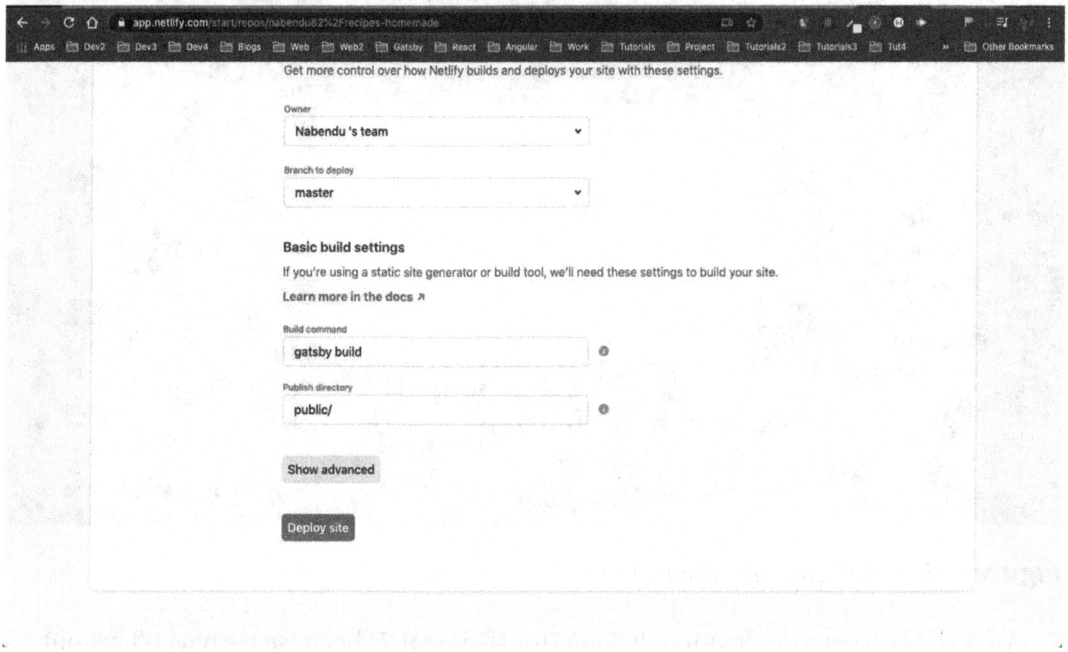

Figure 9-5. *Build*

On the next screen, click Site settings and then scroll a bit down, to change the site name (Figure 9-6).

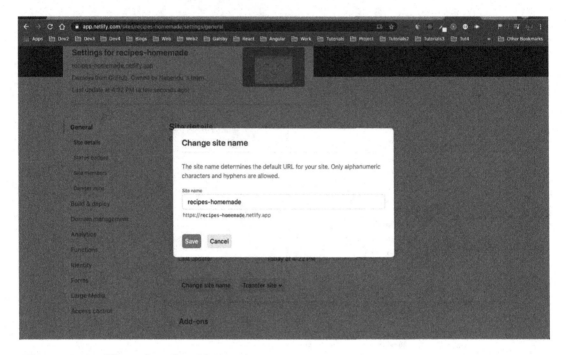

Figure 9-6. Changing the site name

We will soon get a deployment failed error (Figure 9-7) because we haven't yet put the environment variables in Netlify.

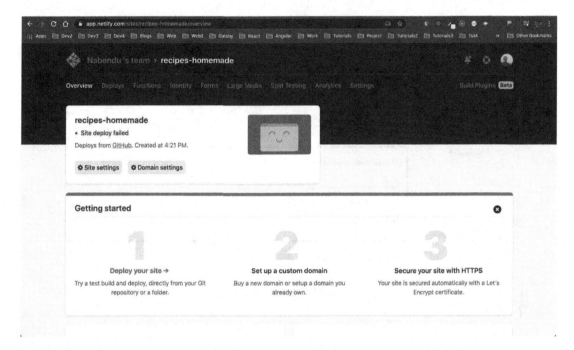

Figure 9-7. *Deployment failed*

Now, click Site settings and then Build & deploy. After that, scroll down until you find the Environment variables section (Figure 9-8).

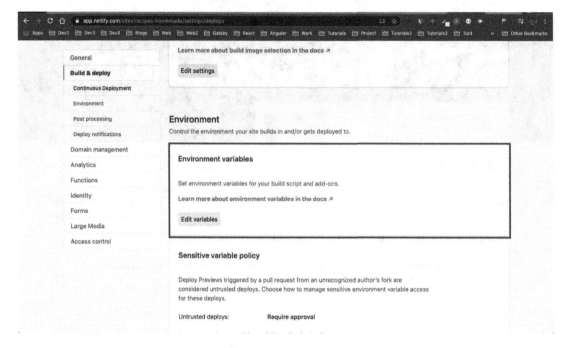

Figure 9-8. *Environment variables*

Click Edit variables and add all variables, with values from our `.env` file. One thing to notice is that the `FIREBASE_PRIVATE_KEY` should appear without double quotes (Figure 9-9).

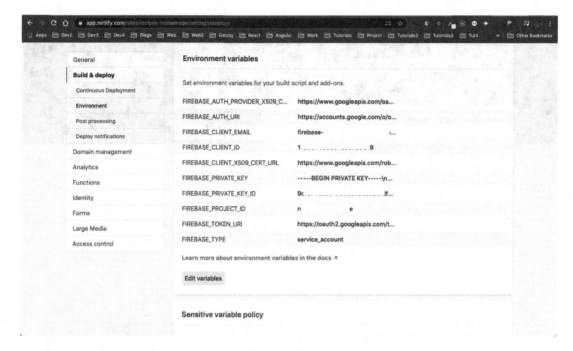

Figure 9-9. *Listing of environment variables*

After that, select Deploys and then click Trigger deploy. Click Clear cache and deploy site (Figure 9-10).

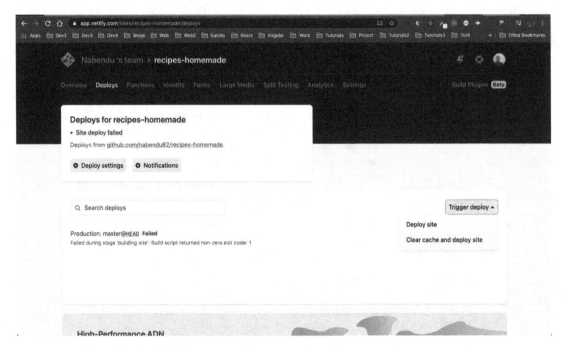

Figure 9-10. *Deploying the site*

Our deployment was successful this time, as indicated in Figure 9-11.

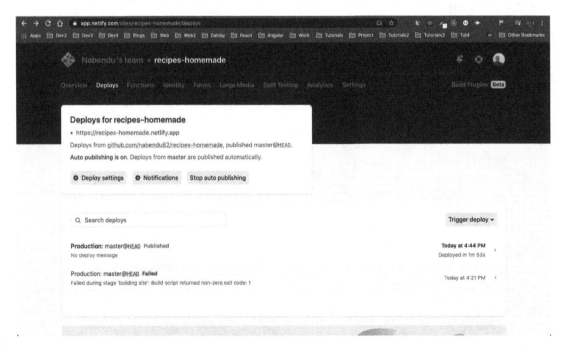

Figure 9-11. *Successful deployment*

Now our site is live, as shown in Figure 9-12, at `https://recipes-homemade.netlify.app/`.

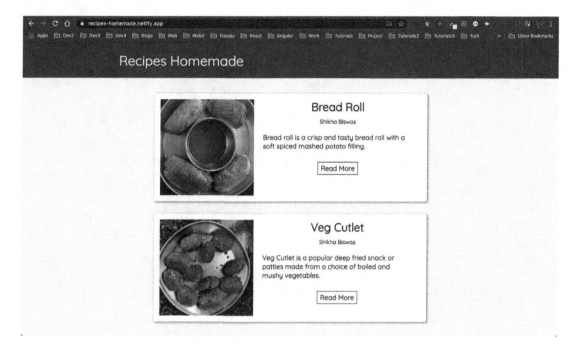

Figure 9-12. *Live site*

Summary

In this chapter, we added environment variables and then successfully deployed our site to Netlify. In the next chapter, we will add the Disqus commenting system in our site.

CHAPTER 10

Adding Disqus Commenting System

In the previous chapter, we added environment variables and then successfully deployed our site to Netlify. In this chapter, we will put a commenting system in place. To do so, we will be using Disqus, a networked community platform used all over the Web. With Disqus, your website gains a feature-rich commenting system complete with social network integration, advanced administration and moderation options, and other extensive community functions.

First, though, we need to make two small changes.

1. The summary of each recipe can be a bit long, so I want to show only 100 words on the home page.

2. We are adding a helper function, `summarySlice`, and returning the sliced string plus three dots.

Modifying the Home Page

To modify the home page, navigate to the `index.js` file and make the changes shown in bold in Listing 10-1.

Listing 10-1. `index.js`

```
const IndexPage = (props) => {
  const summarySlice = (str) => {
    return str.slice(0,100) + "...";
  }
```

© Nabendu Biswas 2021
N. Biswas, *Advanced Gatsby Projects*, https://doi.org/10.1007/978-1-4842-6640-3_10

```
  return (
    <Layout>
      <SEO title="Home" />
      <AllRecipes>
        {props.data.allRecipe.edges.map(edge => (
            <article className="card" key={edge.node.id}>
            <div className="image">
              <Image fluid={edge.node.localImage.childImageSharp.fluid} />
            </div>
            <div className="info">
              <h2>{edge.node.name}</h2>
              <h5>{edge.node.cook.name}</h5>
              <p>{edge.node.summary && summarySlice(edge.node.summary)}</p>
              <Link to={`/recipe/${edge.node.id}`} className="link">read
              more</Link>
            </div>
            </article>
        ))}
      </AllRecipes>
    </Layout>
  )
}
```

index.js

Now, our home page looks like Figure 10-1.

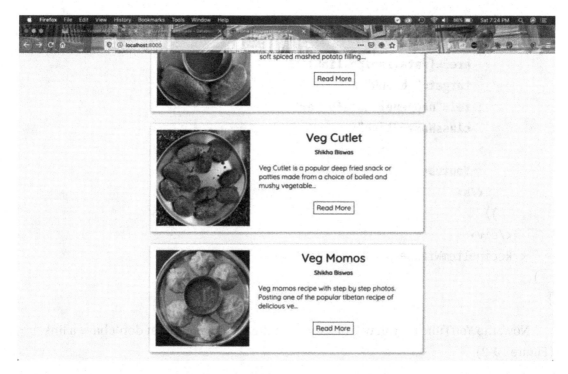

Figure 10-1. *Home page after changes*

Next, some of the recipes don't have a YouTube link, as my wife already knew how to make them. Therefore, open `recipeTemplate.js` and add the conditional rendering of the YouTube button. The updated content for the file is shown in bold in Listing 10-2.

Listing 10-2. `recipeTemplate.js`

```
const RecipeTemplate = ({ data }) => {
  return (
    <RecipeItemWrapper>
      <Link to="/" className="link">
        back to all recipes
      </Link>
      <div className="info">
        <h1>{data.recipe.name}</h1>
        <h4>{data.recipe.cook.name}</h4>
        <Image fluid={data.recipe.localImage.childImageSharp.fluid} />
        <p>{data.recipe.summary}</p>
```

```
      {data.recipe.link && (
        <a
          href={data.recipe.link}
          target="_blank"
          rel="noopener noreferrer"
          className="link"
        >
          Youtube
        </a>
      )}
    </div>
  </RecipeItemWrapper>
)
}
```

Now, the YouTube button will not show on the recipe pages that don't have a link (Figure 10-2).

Veg momos recipe with step by step photos. Posting one of the popular tibetan recipe of delicious vegetable momos or dim sum made from scratch. Making dim sum takes quite a good amount of time. so when you have enough time to spare, then make them. If you have a helping hand, then the time will reduce. But If you do everything on your own, it takes about 1.5 to 2 hrs, depending on your working speed and the gadgets you have in your kitchen.

Figure 10-2. *Recipe with no YouTube link*

Next, we will add Disqus to our site.

Adding Disqus

To add Disqus, we need to install `gatsby-plugin-disqus`. The details of the plug-in can be found at `https://www.gatsbyjs.org/packages/gatsby-plugin-disqus/?=disqus`.

First stop `gatsby develop` on the terminal and install the plug-in with the following command.

```
npm install --save gatsby-plugin-disqus
```

Now, navigate to the Disqus site (Figure 10-3) at `https://disqus.com/`.

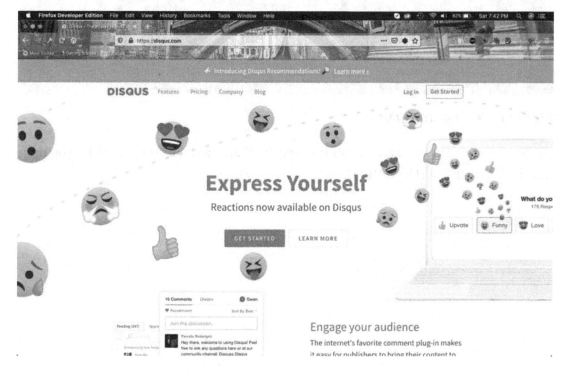

Figure 10-3. *Disqus home page*

After signing up with a Google account, you will see the screen shown in Figure 10-4. Here I chose I want to install Disqus on my site.

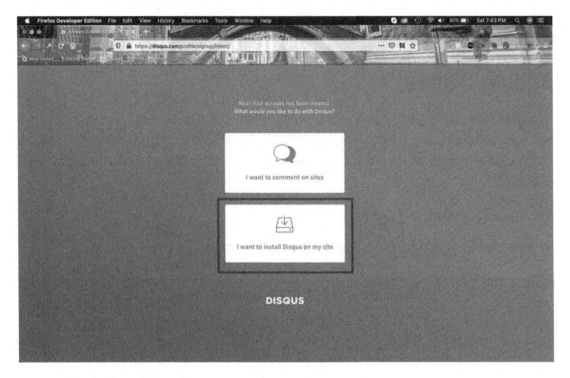

Figure 10-4. *Installing Disqus*

Next, we need to enter a value for the Website Name and the Category. After you do that, click Create Site (Figure 10-5).

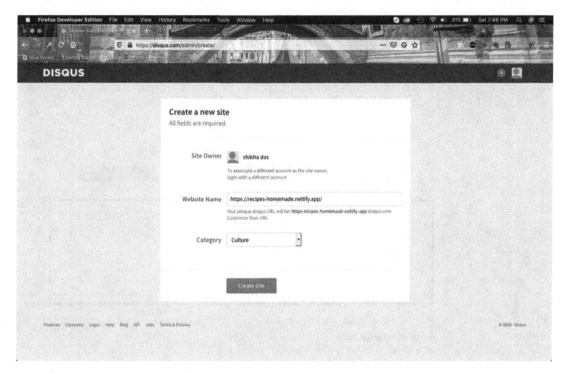

Figure 10-5. *Creating a new site*

After that, click Subscribe Now for the basic, ad-supported, free version of Disqus (Figure 10-6).

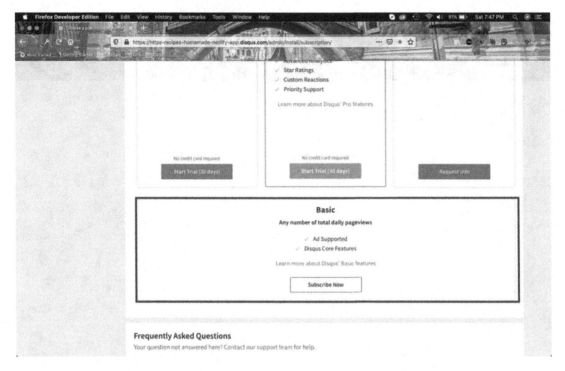

Figure 10-6. *Basic free version*

Next, click the Configure Disqus tab, as our site is not on any of the platforms listed (Figure 10-7).

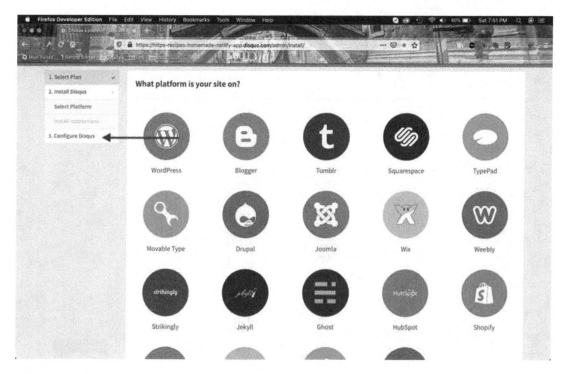

Figure 10-7. *Configure Disqus*

Next, add some basic information and click Complete Setup (Figure 10-8).

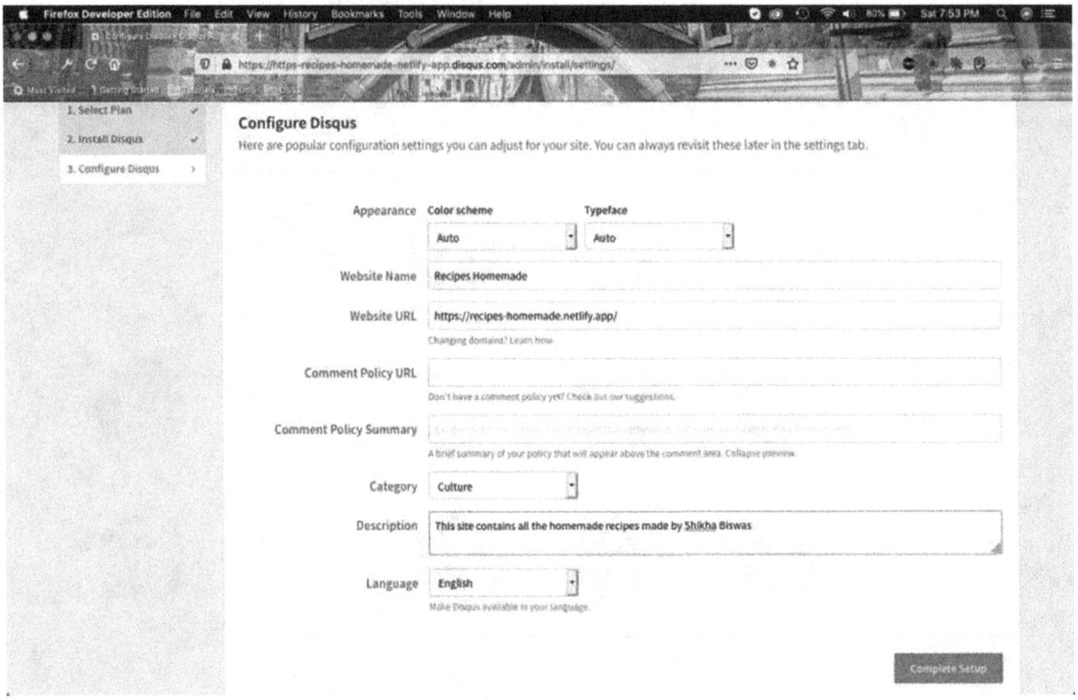

Figure 10-8. *Completing the setup*

Next, click on the Settings tab and copy down the website shortname, which we are going to use in the next step (Figure 10-9).

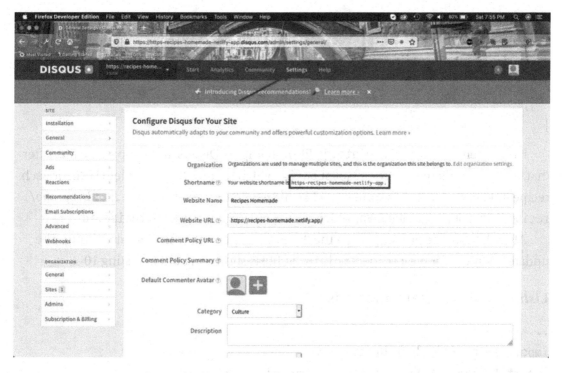

Figure 10-9. *Copy the website shortname*

Next, open the `gatsby-config.js` file and add the plug-in with the website shortname from the preceding step. The updated content for the file is shown in bold in Listing 10-3.

Listing 10-3. `gatsby-config.js`

```
module.exports = {
...
  {
    resolve: `gatsby-plugin-remote-images`,
    options: {
      nodeType: 'Recipe',
      imagePath: 'imageUrl',
    },
  },
  {
    resolve: `gatsby-plugin-disqus`,
```

```
      options: {
          shortname: `https-recipes-homemade-netlify-app`
      }
    }
  ],
}
```

Now, open the recipeTemplate.js file and import Disqus at the top of the file. After that, add the configuration for disqusConfig, which requires the complete URL for each recipe link. In our case, it is something like https://recipes-homemade.netlify.app/ recipe/lQFRBdDWXpUde6HoVbVn, which we are creating using data.recipe.id.

After that, we are passing this in the Disqus component, which we are calling. The updated content for the recipeTemplate.js file is shown in bold in Listing 10-4.

Listing 10-4. recipeTemplate.js

```
...
import Image from "gatsby-image";
import { Disqus } from "gatsby-plugin-disqus";

const RecipeItemWrapper = styled.section`
...
..
`;

const RecipeTemplate = ({ data }) => {
  const url = "https://recipes-homemade.netlify.app/recipe/";
  const blogIdentity = data.recipe.id;
  let disqusConfig = {
      url: `${url}${blogIdentity}`,
      identifier: blogIdentity,
      title: data.recipe.name
  }

  return (
    <RecipeItemWrapper>
      <Link to="/" className="link">
        back to all recipes
      </Link>
```

```
    <div className="info">
    ...
    </div>
    <Disqus config={disqusConfig} />
  </RecipeItemWrapper>
 )
}
```

It's time to push this code to GitHub for automatic deployment to Netlify. The deployment was successful and the commenting system is up on our site (Figure 10-10).

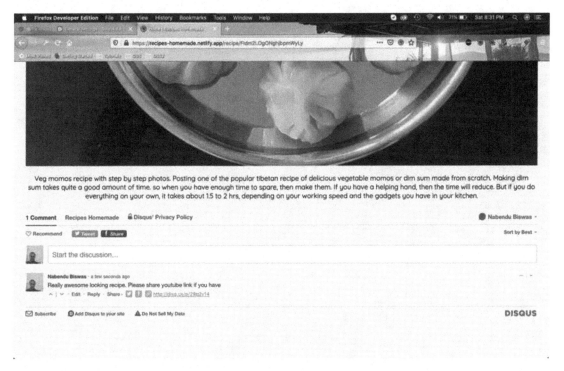

Figure 10-10. *Commenting system*

Summary

This completes the recipe site that I built for my wife. She will soon update all the recipes that she has made recently. I hope you liked the series and learned to use Gatsby with Firebase. You can find the code for this site in the GitHub repo at `https://github.com/nabendu82/recipes-homemade`.

Index

A

Add Menu, 105
    add item, 111
    file selector, 107
    menu item, 106
    published item, 110
    publishing draft, 109
    upload file, 108
API keys, 112–114
    access tokens, 122
    data, 116
    environmental variables, 121
    menu, 115
    Netlify, 119, 120

B

Banner components, 41
    contact page, 46
    default props, 41
    home page, 43, 44
    menu page, 48
    page with text, 45
    updated content, 42–44
Button component, 48
    home page, 51
    style, 49
    utils folder, 49

C

Contentful, (*see* Content modeling)
Content modeling
    add field, 99
    add space, 93
    app, 90
    complete code, 127
    confirm selection, 96
    creation, 87
    desktop screen, 129
    details, 98
    explore button, 88
    free space, 94
    image field, 103
    ingredients
        field, 102
    mobile screen, 130
    price field, 101
    product display, 126
    project, 89
    project space, 92
    save, 104
    settings
        general, 91
        space, 91
    show items, 122, 123
    space home, 97
    space name, 95

© Nabendu Biswas 2021
N. Biswas, *Advanced Gatsby Projects*, https://doi.org/10.1007/978-1-4842-6640-3

Printed in the United States
by Baker & Taylor Publisher Services